REFLECTING
ON THE
WORD
OF THE
LORD

Rev. Randolph Kesler

ARPress
ILLUMINATING IDEAS.
EMPOWERING VOICES

ARPress
45 Dan Road Suite 5
Canton MA 02021
Hotline: 1(888) 821-0229
Fax: 1(508) 545-7580

Ordering Information:

Quantity sales. Special discounts are available on quantity purchases by corporations, associations, and others. For details, contact the publisher at the address above.

Printed in the United States of America.
ISBN-13:   Softcover   979-8-89330-971-3
               eBook   979-8-89330-972-0
Library of Congress Control Number: 2024902537

TABLE OF CONTENTS

Preface

A pastor who continues to read and study the Word of God following his or her graduation from seminary, ordination, and installation into a pastorate develops certain themes and interests which cannot be well-developed without some time away from the rigorous schedule of pastoral duties. I have found across my years of ministry that I have introduced several topics in preaching and teaching which beckon me to explore them more deeply.

I intend this study to be devotional for the reader. As I reflect on these passages of Scripture, I invite you to reflect in the Spirit on the written Word. I invite you to be surprised by the wondrous beauty and the divine wisdom of God as you submit yourself to trusting the truthfulness of the Word, the ultimate truth therein presented, whereby you and I may enjoy blessing for the living of our days and security in Christ for our journeys throughout eternity in the presence of the Lord and his people in the redeemed creation.

I lay no claim to superior insight in the Word, for I do not possess that. I do possess what the Lord has given me in the course of my years of study and obedience to him.

I have no doubt that in the next few pages, you may be scratching your intellectual head wondering what in the world is this man talking about. I reflect on some of the same subjects repeatedly, not because I don't have interest in anything else but because the Spirit seems to keep me focused on these at this point.

So, my intention for the use of this document is for you to think, to study, to hear what I have said based on the scripture passage considered, asking the Lord's instruction and wisdom for you as you read. This permits the reader to begin the practice of reflecting not necessarily on what I have written but on the text from which I have taken my thoughts. By this means, you will give the Spirit time to speak to you, to inform you, and lead you.

My second intention is to fill a void in the world of devotional readings. I hope this can be enjoyed and may be beneficial to the local pastor as well as for the devoted Christian, both of whom on a regular basis sit in their prayer closets and seek a warmer and firmer relationship with their heavenly Father.

Reflecting

I call this deeper exploration "reflecting." Reflecting is purposefully chosen because as a present participle, it expresses an action that continues from the present into the future as opposed to a past completed action. Had I wanted to express the past action of my study of the Christian Scriptures, I would have used the noun reflection.

This study will contain reflections, to be sure, but reflecting means to me that the study of Scripture is an ongoing action carried out by a committed Christian who shows his or her love for the Word of God by the action of continually reflecting upon the Word either in concentrated study or as one moves throughout her or his day with a certain text for consideration.

Secondly, it is my experience that as I have given myself to the study of a passage of scripture, the Spirit continues to speak to me informing me of new truths and applying a variety of approaches to the passage considered. In other words, the study of a particular passage in the written Word never ends for the preacher or teacher or Christian who will remain open continually in a spirit of expectation. I am reminded of the pastor who, over forty years of ministry, had preached his way through the Bible; therefore, I am told he retired because he had said all he could say. I don't find that approach a satisfactory one for me. As I work on sermons from week to week, I am often adding to or reemphasizing some point in my mind even up to and including the moment of preaching.

I have friends in the church who tell me they no longer need to study a certain biblical book because they studied it once, and they understand it. Such an approach to the biblical text indicates a rigid and fixed view as though the Spirit of God has no further word to say or message to bring to inform our living as time passes. This attitude hampers Christian growth and hardens the believer to the fresh winds of the Spirit. It reminds me of having eaten steak or salad as a child and determining that, because I have enjoyed this one steak or one salad, I have no further need to taste another because any subsequent steak or salad will be the same.

So, for me, reflecting indicates the ongoing, continual interaction of the child of God with the Word of God in sensitivity to the Spirit of God. It is certainly not a one-time experience but a repeated, recurrent, and persistent turning of oneself to the Lord for inspiration and guidance, instruction and authority for one's life.

Meditating on Scripture

As the people of God under the leadership of Joshua prepared to take the land of Canaan as their promised inheritance to Abraham and his descendants, the Lord gave these instructions to Joshua, "Do not let this Book of the Law depart from your mouth; *meditate on it day and night,* so that you may be careful to do everything written in it. Then you will be prosperous and successful" (Joshua 1:8).

So *meditating* carries the idea of reflecting, the "act of thoughtful deliberation with the implication of speaking to oneself" (NIV *Exhaustive Concordance,* 2047, Goodrick and Kohlenberger III). Thoughtful deliberation to inform oneself is the foundational, faithful approach of any serious follower of Jesus Christ regarding their approach to the Holy Scripture.

We find an additional shade of meaning for meditating in Psalm 48:9, "Within your temple, O God, we meditate on your unfailing love." This different Hebrew word (NIV *Exhaustive Concordance,* 1948, Goodrick and Kohlenberger III)) includes the desire of the "medita-tor" to incorporate into her or his life the idea or ideal being contemplated (e.g., in this case, God's unfailing love).

Therefore, in these few pages, I invite your contemplation of Scripture with me. These thoughts, of course, are not mine alone, for what I think and feel and do is the end result of a lifetime of studying God's Word in conjunction with the writings and teachings of others. I am gratified if the Spirit has given me any insight in these passages which will open to the reader some clearer understanding and deeper Christian growth.

 One purpose in presenting this is to encourage you to reflect on the Word. Immerse yourself in the Word you read, and store it in your heart and mind, then as you go about your daily walk, the Spirit of God will enhance your understanding and inform your plans for living in Christ.

Lastly, I remind my congregation regularly in preaching, teaching, and in governing the church that the study of the written Word of God is absolutely required for Christian growth. My

Presbyterian background teaches me that in the study of the written Word, the living Word (the risen Christ) comes into our hearts and transforms our lives by molding us into the image of the Son of God which gives us life.

Presuppositions

I am blessed to have incorporated into my life certain presuppositions which will undergird my interpretation, my reflections on these passages of scripture.

First, I write as a Christian to Christians. I have no desire to make in-depth comparisons of Christianity with other religions. I will say that the Christian Scriptures, including the Hebrew Old Testament and the Greek New Testament, speak for themselves needing no authentication by me or anyone else. One need to only read them and reflect, committing oneself to the God who gave them to us, to find them sufficient for the abundant life offered in Jesus Christ.

Secondly, I write in the mainstream of classical Christianity. I have no desire to be controversial. I have found that those who wish to amaze or shock an audience with some doctrine or theory which has been recycled recently by an ill-informed press is generally not Christian and not in the mainstream of the church's doctrine. For example, the Gnostic gospels which have recently enjoyed resuscitation in novels and, in a limited fashion, by some fringe scholars, were ancient books thoroughly examined by informed Christian leaders 1600–1800 years ago. These early Christian bishops, who examined the Gnostic gospels, were disciples of disciples of the apostles and, in some cases, disciples of the apostles themselves. Moreover, every contributor to the New Testament canon from Paul to Mark to John and Peter, in some way, found these Gnostics infiltrating the infant congregations for the purpose of distorting doctrine and primarily, for the purpose of dividing the church. These teachers had a different gospel particularly relating to creation, salvation, and the supremacy of Jesus Christ as the Son of God and "the only name under heaven given among men by which we may be saved" (Acts 4:12).

Thirdly, I believe that the Christian Scriptures (the Bible) are authoritative as the Word of God to human beings. This means that the Christian must submit to the authority of God in his or her life as revealed in the written Word. In Christian belief, the only other authorities available are the church traditions and the Spirit of God. The teaching of the church must be based on the authority of Scripture or else they can become tainted by human error. Likewise, the message someone receives from the Spirit must be tested: the Spirit will never direct someone to believe or do anything which disagrees with the written Word. Therefore, we must study the Scripture to ascertain God's will for us as his children. Church tradition such as the writings of the fathers and the adopted confessions of faith and creeds by the church are extremely valuable and need to be compared with Scripture, but they must never succeed to the level of scriptural authority since they are more susceptible to the human imprint.

The proper balance, it seems to me, regarding the authority of Scripture is that God reveals himself to us in the written Word which is inspired by the Spirit of God and, by the same Spirit, in the study of the written Word, we find the supreme revelation: the living Word who is Jesus Christ our savior and Lord.

Fourth, I believe that Scripture is "God-breathed," inspired by the Spirit and written by the direction of God. Over a period of almost four hundred years, the church by worship and teaching received the Old Testament immediately since the early Christians were Jewish in background, and what we now call the New Testament was adopted as the canon of Scripture by around AD 400. Directed by the Spirit, the early Christian congregations witnessed to the self-sufficiency of the apostolic writings as God's truth for them and for all Christ's followers. As they had read the Old Testament in synagogues as Jews, they added to those readings the letters of Paul and others including the early gospels. So, by the practice and faith of the early congregations, the New Testament books were then selected as authoritative and inspired by the Spirit. The Bible we now have does not contain all the truth that is absolute (God alone is that truth), but it does contain all the truth any human being needs to come to a knowledge of God as Savior and Lord and to serve as an authoritative and sufficient guide for us as we live our lives in Christ.

Fifth, I believe in the unity of Scripture. The Old and New Testaments are equally inspired by the Spirit and interpreted rightly, stand as a unity of the truth and love of the Lord in his world. By this, I mean that the God of the Old Testament is the same God in the New Testament who is the Father of Jesus Christ. This, being just one example, is an extremely significant example. In today's church, it seems to me, we have reached a crisis because I hear very little proclamation of gospel from the Old Testament. Such a lack of Old Testament interpretation belies an insufficient understanding and an almost heretical approach to the doctrine of Scripture.

Lastly, let me mention that I have a high view of the authority of Scripture. By now, you should know that. There are two convictions I bring with me whenever I study a text. One is the conviction that if I don't understand something in Scripture, it is my lack of study and training. No man or woman, regardless of training and education or lack thereof, has the right to defame or distort the Word of God acting as self-sanctioning authority. So, if something does not seem to make sense to me, I learn to wait and pray and study until the Spirit informs me if he so desires. Sometimes, after reflecting for some time, greater understanding comes; in other situations, I continue without additional insight. But under no circumstances will I ever believe that the Scripture is lacking; it is I who lack.

The second conviction which accompanies me as I study the text is that the text is not sacred and holy in and of itself. These words, no matter how precious they are to me, are meant to lead me to the living Lord—the living Word—Jesus Christ. Mary A. Lathbury, a child of the Chautauqua devotional movement of the late nineteenth century, composed the great hymn "Break Thou the Bread of Life." A favorite New Testament professor of mine reminded us often that the study of the Word is not the ultimate goal in and of itself. The ultimate purpose for studying the sacred text is that, by so doing, we are brought into the presence of the risen Christ, the living Word.

Break Thou the bread of life, Dear Lord to me,

As Thou didst break the loaves beside the sea;

Beyond the sacred page I seek Thee Lord;

My spirit pants for Thee, O Living Word.

"Open Thy Word of Truth that I may see

Thy message written clear and plain for me;

Then in sweet fellowship, *walking with Thee,*

Thine Image on my life engraved will be.

"O send Thy Spirit, Lord, now unto me,

That He may touch my eyes and make me see;

Show me the *truth concealed within Thy Word,*

And in Thy Book revealed I see the Lord.

Now that says it better than I. As we *reflect,* we do so in the belief that the written Word is inspired and interpreted by the Spirit of God as he reveals to us the living Lord and applies the truth of God to remake us in his image.

Now, I have told you some of what I believe about the Scripture, which I adopt as the foundation of my life which leads me to the reality which alone is the way, the truth and the life, even Jesus Christ my Lord. What are your foundations, your ultimate truths? On whom or what do you depend for eternal truth and ultimate destiny? Is it the teaching of the written Word? Is it what you experience in your life each day? Is it some spirituality which others have mentioned to you? Is it what you heard some teacher or preacher, or parent say? How do you know it is right and true?

Every human being must have a foundation on which they depend for truth beyond themselves. Which reality we choose will make all the difference in life and in death.

1

Beginnings

Reflecting on Genesis 1:1–2

"In the beginning God created the heavens and the earth. Now the earth was formless and empty, darkness was over the surface of the deep, and the Spirit of God was hovering over the waters."

This text tells us that creation has a beginning, a starting place; that before the beginning, God is. Only God.

Creation is about beginnings, and it is the teaching of Scripture that although God's creative work is complete and perfect, God's work of creation is also ongoing. In some sense, God never stops creating. Let's trace it this way.

In Genesis 1, God creates the universe as our text indicates, the heavens and the earth. In verse 26 of the first chapter of Genesis, God creates humankind. Humankind differs from land or sea or birds of the air, for humankind are created in the image of God. Even though we are related to other animal life forms for we are created on the sixth day just as they are, we are turned toward God for we have his image within us.

Another beginning occurs when God provides grace for sinful humanity before the judgment of the flood. He calls Noah to build the ark for the preservation of the original creation. So Noah, by grace and by his trust in the Word of the Lord, becomes a restored image-bearer for the Lord; he walks with God (prays and fellowships), and his heart is turned toward God's purposes (committed to do the will of the Lord). Yet, following the deliverance to safety in the ark following the flood, Noah and his family exhibit a prideful response to the loving grace of God, and his extended family stretching all the way to the Tower of Babel abuse their intellectual and technological God-given gifts to then construct the tower in defiance of the Lord that they may "build ourselves a city, with a tower that reaches to the heavens, so that we may make a name for ourselves and not be scattered over the face of the whole earth" (Genesis 11:4).

Hence, another beginning is prepared by the Lord in Genesis 12 with the call of Abraham to follow where the Lord will lead him—that is, Abraham must learn to live by faith in God, trusting in his promises of land, of babies, and of nation status. When God called Abraham, he had no land in the place God led him, no babies through whom descendants would come; and certainly, no nation, simply one family.

Moreover, all this will be accomplished because Abraham learns to trust God. Abraham will become the father of the people of God who respond to him in faith and who live by his covenant in a mutual relationship. And the reason for this creation of faith response toward God centered in one family or people? It is that this family will bring blessing to every other family or nation of the earth; they offer God's grace and love to them asking them to respond to the Lord in faith and walk with him in obedience. Please review those promises in Genesis 12:1–3.

Beginnings of the People of God

A. Birth – Exodus.

In the Exodus (Exodus 1–14) from Egypt, we find the birth of the people of God. This is a fresh beginning because over a period of four hundred years, Abraham's family was first preserved by and then enslaved to the Pharaohs of Egypt. We may think of this as their conception and gestation period in the womb of God's grace during the time of a very difficult pregnancy.

When the Lord delivers them passing through the Red Sea on dry ground and, at the same time, destroys the Egyptian army in their pursuit, we should think of the Red Sea crossing as the birth of the children of Israel.

B. Covenant – Lifestyle.

A fifth moment of creative beginning occurs when Moses brings the people to Mount Sinai and there receives them in grace and offers them the benefits of their salvation in the Exodus. It's as though God is saying to them, "Since I saved you, since I preserved you against the mightiest empire in world history [Egypt] at that point in time, I want now to offer you an invitation written by my own hand on stone tablets. [Please notice this is the written Word of God.] I have saved you for my purposes, and here is how you may benefit most from the new life I am offering you."

The idea of covenant is one of the singular concepts which binds the Scriptures together as a unit. In the ancient world, nations or groups would agree together to the conditions of a treaty for their mutual benefit, much the same as we do today. Generally, there were two parties making agreements, and usually the covenant agreement followed a war between the two groups, only one of course being the victor. Therefore, the victorious party laid down the conditions which would govern the relationship between the two nations. The loser nation became a dependent state to the winner nation. The dependent state would pay annual tribute to the victor in the form of produce or livestock or even jurisdiction over various cities and, not the least, taxes. In return, the dependent state was due protection from the victorious state if a third nation should attack them.

When this covenant idea is applied to the Lord and his "nation to be," the Israelites whom he has just freed from Egyptian domination, the Lord is the victor, and the Israelites are the dependent ones. God is under no obligation to give them anything; God is in total control. The Israelites have no rights by virtue of their goodness or actions.

C. Covenant is grace.

Therefore, God comes to them in total grace.

1. First, offering himself by the disclosure of his name *Yahweh* "I Am Who I Am" (Exodus 3:14).

2. Then, he delivers them from slavery to other nations and their gods.

3. Then, he brings them to Sinai, where he first appeared to Moses that the people may know the Lord as Moses knows him.

In summary, the Ten Words (Commandments) are God's covenant agreement with his people for their benefit to help them live in such a way that he will receive their glory and praise, and they will be blessed with peace and grace and security. That is the covenant God made with them. The Ten Words are God's instrument of grace offered by his love, anchored in his goodness for the total blessing of his people who trust him as Lord.

As for the people, they are sinful, disobedient, rebellious human beings to whom the Lord in his grace has extended forgiveness, mercy, love, and his personal presence to accompany them all the days of their lives.

The Ten Words then are an instruction manual for life for people of faith. And what is the response God expects from the people? What is their part of covenant? It is to give him their total allegiance in worship and service and to live in heartfelt agape love (doing the best for all in every situation). The first four words are concerned with the people's response to the Lord who has saved them, and the final six with their love for their fellowmen. In short, they are to act toward others as the Lord has acted toward them in grace, mercy, and accountable love.

Simplified, God is saying that he has brought them back from certain enslavement and death in Egypt to freedom and, by the Exodus, has given them the joy of personal liberty and autonomy under the constitutional and covenantal rule of God.

Is the Covenant Meant to be a Law or a Prescription?

I believe there is general misinterpretation at this point particularly concerning the expression of the Ten Words as law. Two Hebrew words are used for "commandments" as in the Ten Commandments. One of them is quite correctly translated as commandment, but an alternative possibility is the word "prescription or instruction" (Exodus 20:6; Deuteronomy 5:10)

I believe prescription or instruction is closer to the contextual meaning for the written word given by the Lord at Sinai.

The second translation is "word" as in the Ten Words (Exodus 34:28; Deuteronomy 4:13). Note that both the author of Exodus and Deuteronomy use both Hebrew words for "prescription" and "word" which is rendered "commandment" in most translations of the Bible.

The Motivation for Fulfilling the Covenant Is Thanksgiving.

By seeking to change the force of the word *commandment*, I am not seeking to soften the need for obedience or heading toward the Ted Turner approach of some years ago calling them the "Ten Suggestions." I am only trying to capture the sense of grace which pervades this text and the broader biblical context. As the centuries pass and humankind becomes more hardened to grace, a works faith pervades Israel. By the time of Jesus and Paul, there developed a secondary interpretation of the Ten Words which won the day. It was that at Sinai, the Lord demanded such obedience for salvation; that is, we could earn salvation by keeping these laws. Since that was not possible, though the Pharisees tried, salvation had to be obtained according to Paul and others by trusting Christ's righteousness as our own and laying our sins upon him in his death on the cross.

So notice the contextual truth as the Ten Words are presented at Sinai (page 13). When the Lord brings them to Sinai and offers them the Ten Commandments, he is granting them the grace of discipleship. "What do you want to do for me since I have saved you? Formerly, Pharaoh was your master; now I am your Master, but most importantly, I am your Lord. In offering you these directives for purposeful living, I am giving you the opportunity to share in my life."

A Thankful Lifestyle

The Ten Commandments are not intended to be understood as laws, not even as the supreme law but as grace words for living. They are intended to be the bedrock commitment for the structuring of society and for a trusting marriage between the Lord and his people. Perhaps, at this point, a New Testament illustration will help.

In the New Testament, in Galatians 5:22-23, Paul gives us the same understanding of grace life from an intimate and personal point of view. The individual maturing Christian is to demonstrate in his or her life the following characteristics which Paul views as the fruit of the Spirit: love, joy, peace, patience, kindness, goodness, faithfulness, gentleness and self-control. Against such there is no law.

Each of us should strive to bring our lives into conformity with these Christ-like attitudes since, after all, we have become the children of God through grace and faith in Jesus Christ. The fruit of the Spirit in this text parallels the Ten Words in Exodus 20.

In the same way at Sinai, the Lord instructs his people in the ways of grace which will bring them peace and purpose as they serve him as master and Lord. They received salvation in the Exodus event. The Ten Words must always be understood contextually which is this: first, the Lord saved his people by the Exodus then offers them the invitation to successful living by adherence to these Ten Commandments. The context was not, and this is where much theology has run aground, that the Lord saved them; now at Sinai, they must do these things to keep themselves in a right relationship with him.

The Lord saves his own; He conceives them from the call of Abraham, the sojourn in Canaan, the enslavement in Egypt— that is the *womb of their pregnancy.*

Then in the Exodus, the Lord gives *birth to them.*

Then at Sinai, with the invitation to receive and obey the Ten Commandments, the Lord offers them the steppingstones with which they may build their lives in walking with him and growing to maturity in him. It is what theologians call sanctification—*it is the child of God living as he or she understands God to live.* He makes them holy. He makes them his own.

This is completely described in Exodus 19:3–6.

Then Moses went up to God and Lord called to him from the mountain and said, "This is what you are to say to the house of Jacob and what you are to tell the people of Israel: You yourselves have seen what I did to Egypt [destruction and plague] and how I carried you on eagle's wings and brought you to Myself [salvation and birth].

Now if you obey Me fully and keep my covenant [invitation to life and relationship with the Lord—the Ten Words), then out of all nations, you will be my treasured possession. [*The people of God will extend his grace to all other peoples.*] Although the whole earth is mine, you will be for Me a kingdom of priests and a holy nation." (*Missionaries consecrated to God's holy purpose in outreach/evangelism*)

Sacred to the Lord

What then does the Lord ask of those whom he saved and who, otherwise, would have died as slaves in Egypt? Read it in Exodus 20:1-17.

And God spoke all these words:

"I am the *Lord* your God, who brought you out of Egypt, out of the land of slavery."

"You shall have no other gods before me."

"You shall not make for yourself an image in the form of anything in heaven above or on the earth beneath or in the waters below. You shall not bow down to them or worship them; for I, the *Lord* your God, am a jealous God, punishing the children for the sin of the parents to the third and fourth generation of those who hate me, but showing love to a thousand generations of those who love me and keep my commandments."

"You shall not misuse the name of the *Lord* your God, for the *Lord* will not hold anyone guiltless who misuses his name."

"Remember the Sabbath day by keeping it holy. Six days you shall labor and do all your work, but the seventh day is a sabbath to the *Lord* your God. On it you shall not do any work, neither you, nor your son or daughter, nor your male or female servant, nor your animals, nor any foreigner residing in your towns. For in six days the *Lord* made the heavens and the earth, the sea, and all that is in them, but he rested on the seventh day. Therefore, the *Lord* blessed the Sabbath day and made it holy."

"Honor your father and your mother, so that you may live long in the land the *Lord* your God is giving you."

"You shall not murder."

"You shall not commit adultery."

"You shall not steal."

"You shall not give false testimony against your neighbor."

"You shall not covet your neighbor's house. You shall not covet your neighbor's wife, or his male or female servant, his ox or donkey, or anything that belongs to your neighbor."

1. *Exclusive worship of the Lord our God.*

Is that too much to ask from the One who brought you freedom from slavery to sin and brought you abundant life?

2. *Spiritual worship of the Lord as personal God* rather than worshipping idols which are carvings or reproductions from created matter. Additionally, the idols can be seen, and Israel's Lord is not visible; we must trust him, living in faith and not by sight in visible manifestations. Throughout Scripture, the point is made to Israel of the folly of worshipping a man-made object in the attempt to worship the creator God—the one who made the substance from which an idol might be made or carved.

3. *Worship the Lord in your heart, personally and intimately* because he has revealed himself by his name, "I am who am." The Lord basically said, "I have opened to you my heart. Now open yours to me. Do not be disrespectful by making a common noun out of the proper noun Yahweh—the Lord by using the name of the Lord casually and superficially.

4. *Worship the Lord regularly and faithfully in set times and places;* that is, worship that is proper, personal, and public.

Service to humankind

Then the Lord graced his people with the foundations of a healthy human society. The cornerstone of life as the Lord designed it is found in a family.

5. *Respect for your father and mother* who are the conduits of the image of God in society. Like God, our parents should be creative, responsible, intimately personal, volitional, communicative, moral, committed, and valued by family and society. After all, they are the image-bearers of the Lord.

6. *Respect all life as holy, particularly human life.*

In no way does this preclude societal restrictions for those who show disrespect for the lives of others. Biblically, all life is sacred; we must honor human life above other life forms. Yet, as stewards of the mandate of creation to exercise dominion (Genesis 1:26), we must learn to rule wisely under the teachings of God, and the basic injunction throughout Scripture is the sanctity of human life. Scripture makes exceptions regarding the taking of life under the rubric of the preservation of society. By the Lord's command in creation to rule over and have dominion over the other creatures, the taking of life is permitted by strict guidelines in situations like self-defense, war, and capital punishment.

7. *Respect the marriage relationship.* Throughout Scripture, the relationship of marriage between woman and man is used to reflect the most holy of all relationships—that of a man or woman with their Lord. Hence, human marriage is meant to be trusting, personally intimate, faithfully practiced, exclusively enjoyed, enduring forever, and lived out daily in agape love. (Agape love is doing the best for someone in every situation in accordance with God's purpose and providence. The husband and wife who practice agape toward each other minimize their problems and enhance their opportunities.)

8. *Respect for private property and personal rights.* This would extend to the government as well as to one's neighbor. Far from being limited to real estate or financial considerations, stealing is forbidden regarding intellectual ideas, the withholding of emotional satisfactions, wasting the time

of our employer, or refusing to give God his due in our lives. A society which loses its respect for the rights and properties of others cannot stand long.

9. *Respect for the truth personally, relationally and in civil testimony.* Lying distorts reality, rationalizes wrongdoing, and leads to disillusionment and despair. When the lie is supported as the truth, basic values are diminished, and society cannot stand long.

10. *Respect for the total human condition of others.*

Coveting is the desire to have what does not belong to you. It is scorning the grace of our lives, the gifts of God to us, and being ungrateful for our place in the world, our position in the community, and the blessings we enjoy. We need to rejoice in the welfare and blessing of others.

The Grace Gifts of Sinai

To me, recasting these Ten Words as grace for living accomplishes two things: By removing the negative demand of "thou shalt not," we may understand these in the grace context in which they were presented concerning the salvation history of the people of God. First came salvation in the Exodus and then follows God like living exhorted and prescribed in the Ten Words. Secondly, it restores to us the positive aspects of the understanding of law. Almost universally, in a Christian religious context, law is understood to set up a standard which judges us. As stated earlier, this becomes the understanding of the Jewish community with the passage of time until, in St. Paul's day, he must deal with law as the "schoolmaster which brings us to Christ," that is, pointing out our failures and turning us to God in repentance.

However, at least an equal and a more historically accurate attitude toward law is found in the Old Testament. We have only to turn to the magnificence of the 119th Psalm.

The Psalmist longs to see "the wonderful things in your law" (119:18) and asks the Lord to be gracious to him through His law (119:29). There is an attitude of adoration and adulation for the law for the writer promises to keep your law and obey your law and to not turn from it (verses 34, 44, 51). In verse 72, we read, "The law from your mouth is more precious to me than thousands of pieces of silver and gold," and in verse 77, "your law is my delight."

Here, then, are some of the successive beginnings of the Lord following his creation of the universe. As with creation, each separate beginning is his act of grace toward us and his desire for goodness to follow us all the days of our lives. Essentially, God desires for us to deal with each other as he has dealt with us—in continuing goodness and love. In particular, the Ten Words are the constitution (rights, privileges, and responsibilities) God gives his people which enumerate his grace and guidance for his children. The concepts are holy and sacred bringing blessing and peace, and coming wholly from the hand of God, they are his grace gifts by which he transforms slaves into friends.

2

Bara

"In the beginning God created the heavens and the earth. Now the earth was formless and empty, darkness was over the surface of the deep, and the Spirit of God was hovering over the waters" (Genesis 1:1–2).

Creation is the work of God. It is *bara*. When the biblical text tells us God created, it always uses the Hebrew word bara. As far as the Scripture is concerned bara or creating is the work of God alone. Bara is never used in Scripture except when God is the subject. If a craftsman makes or creates an object, another word is used, never bara.

The Purpose of Creation Is Redemption

It has been the consistent witness of the church that creation is not an end in and of itself. That is to say, what God created has a larger purpose than the majesty and beauty of matter and space. The larger purpose of the created universe is to serve as the stage in the theater on which the drama of God's ultimate purpose is portrayed: the redemption of humankind, and the restoration of the universe to its splendor (Karl Barth). Perhaps the best scriptural expression of this thought is in Ephesians 1:3f. St. Paul wrote,

Praise be to the God and Father of our Lord Jesus Christ, who has blessed us in the heavenly realms with every spiritual blessing in Christ. For He chose us in Him before the creation of the world to be holy and blameless in his sight. In love He predestined us to be adopted as his sons [and daughters] through Jesus Christ, in accordance with his pleasure and will- to the praise of his glorious grace, which he has freely given us in the One He loves.

And then in verse 11 of the same chapter, "In Him, we were also chosen, having been predestined according to the plan of Him who works out everything in conformity with the purpose of His will."

Therefore, those in Christ have been chosen in God's heart and mind (redeemed) before the creation of the world to be holy and blameless (predestined). Moreover, God, in his sovereign providence, will advance his will and insure his purpose in the world he has created both personally for every individual and cosmically for the entire creation. He will permit the existence of sin and evil, yet God will not allow the destructive destinies of evil and sin to rule and reign forever. They are being checked, and one day, they and their influence will be destroyed.

Creation Is Out of Nothing

Bara means that God creates out of nothing; that is, there is no prehistoric matter which predates God and which he uses to recast the universe. His mode of creation is by word. He speaks the world and all within it into existence by voice and word. The text puts it, "And God said," six times in chapter one, and then in verse 26, "Then God said." The "said" becomes creation by the spoken word of God. What God creates has never before existed.

I find significance that bara is used six times in Genesis 1. In 1:1, "In the beginning God *created*." In 1:21, "So God *created* the great creatures of the sea and every living and moving this with which the water teems...and every winged bird according to its kind." Then in 1:27, "So God *created* man in his own image, in the image of God He *created* him; male and female He *created* them" (three times). Clearly, the author wishes us to understand that there are three characteristics of creation which belong exclusively to God's activity: creation of the universe out of nothing (1:1), the creation of creatures who have some consciousness of their own awareness (1:21) and, at the summit, the creation of humankind which has God's self-awareness (1:27).

Lastly, beyond Genesis, God is the one who can cleanse the human heart and who can create (bara) a pure heart inside us when sin has blighted our lives (Psalm 51:10). And God will create a new heaven and a new earth (Isaiah 65:17) as by grace, he overturns the effects of human sin and restores the earth and heavens to the glory he originally intended. In that day, the people of God will dwell in security and be filled with true purpose as they glorify and enjoy God in his fullness throughout eternity.

Beginning of Wisdom

There are many more beginnings, but we won't look into each of them in such detail. God is the God of beginnings. He is always seeking to bestow grace on his children which always brings them the opportunity for new beginnings in their lives. Sometimes he brings the lives of broken children to an end as with Eli (1 Samuel 3:11–14), and yet he brings about a new beginning with Samuel.

The theme of creation as a beginning is majestically continued in the Wisdom Literature with the breathtaking hymn of wisdom in Proverbs 8. The writer here personifies Wisdom as the guiding force of the provident care and purpose of God. In verse 22f we read:

The Lord brought me forth as the first of his works, before his deeds of old; I was appointed from eternity, from the beginning before the world began. When there were no oceans, I was given birth... I was there when he set the heavens in place... I was the craftsman at his side. I was filled with delight day after day, rejoicing always in his presence, rejoicing in his whole world and delighting in mankind.

Then in Colossians 1, St. Paul describes Jesus's role in creation:

He is the image of the invisible God, the first born over all creation. For by Him all things were created: things in heaven and on earth, visible and invisible, whether thrones or powers or rulers or authorities; all things were created by Him and for Him.

He is before all things, and in Him all things hold together... For God was pleased to have all his fullness dwell in Him, and through Him to reconcile to Himself all things, whether things on earth or things in heaven by making peace through his blood, shed on the cross.

So Jesus is associated with the personified Wisdom in Proverbs. Thus the preexistent Christ is the agent of creation along with the Father and the Spirit in Genesis 1:1–2.

Beginning of the Living Word

And then we come to the earliest gospel in the New Testament, the Gospel according to St. Mark. In the very first verse, Mark gives us the outline of his unparalleled achievement: the first edition of the good news about Jesus. St. Mark is the first to give us the literary form of gospel. He echoes the Genesis text, "The beginning of the gospel about Jesus Christ, the Son of God" (Mark 11:1), and those three names give us the church's understanding of the identity (the who-ness) of Jesus. He is man—Jesus (Mark 1:9). He is earthly/heavenly, conquering anointed bringer of deliverance/salvation—the Messiah (Mark 8:27–29). He is divine man—the Son of God, the ruler of this world, the bringer of victory and life (Mark 15:39).

Jesus from Creation to Recreation

The life and ministry of Jesus is indeed the supreme moment of the first creation (Ephesians 1:4, we were chosen in him before the creation of the world) and the supreme moment of the new creation for God the Creator, as Jesus, has now become grace entering into time, matter, and space. Everything since the fall of humankind has been moving toward this mighty crescendo. What God did in creation by word, "And God said," now becomes personal, holy Word of God in the man Jesus as he so often says in the gospels, "Truly, truly, I say to you."

Next, St. John takes up the theme of the beginning creation and, along with the writer of Proverbs, brings into focus the eternity of Christ.

In the beginning was the Word, and Word was with God, and the Word was God. He was with God in the beginning. Through Him all things were made; without Him nothing was made that has been made. In Him was life, and that life was the light of men. (John 1:1–4)

The Significance of the Incarnation

In the first letter of first John, the apostle continues his theme:

"That which [*he who*] was from the beginning, which we have heard, which we have seen with our own eyes, which we have looked at and our hands have touched. This we proclaim concerning the Word of Life" (1 John 1:1).

This passage is extremely significant in its expression of the knowledge the apostle had of what the Lord Jesus's life and ministry has been from the beginning. There is continuity with the ancient creation described in Genesis. The man Jesus came to exist in human form about 4 BC, but God the Son has always existed with the Father and the Spirit before the beginning.

Yet this God who is without beginning and has no end graciously entered into human life to show us who God is and what God wants from his people. The apostle, writing sixty years following the death, resurrection, and ascension of Jesus to the Father, thinks back now across those years. Perhaps he remembered the day he first saw Jesus when John the Baptizer pointed him and Andrew to Jesus saying, "Behold the Lamb of God, who takes away the sin of the world" (John 1:29). In verse 39 of that chapter, John tells us the first time he met Jesus—about the tenth hour; that is four o'clock in the afternoon. He certainly could have told us where he was when he met Jesus and what he was wearing, the color of his eyes and hair. John knew Jesus in the flesh and, now as an old man in his eighties, he longed to know him sixty years later as he had known him in his youth.

But it was not the physical characteristics for which John longed; it was Jesus's essence. He had heard Jesus's words, his speech, his message, and it had taken hold of him and transformed him and made him a new man—a man who would never be the same again. He had seen him with his own eyes; this was no second or third-hand story from another. John had seen him, gazed upon him, wondered about him and sought to fathom his grace. And John had touched him. Jesus was real, not some spirit from another world, not some ghostly, unearthly being who pretended to be a man. He was reality and truth, dressed in the garb of human flesh.

And that is the journey of beginnings from the original creation in Genesis 1 to the life and ministry of Jesus in 1 John 1. "And God said" became "the Word became flesh and dwelt among us, full of grace and truth" (John 1:14). He is the one who came from the Father, his one and only one.

And lastly, in Revelation 21, we have the completed promise of the creational beginnings offered in Genesis. "In the beginning" always implies an "ending." But with our God, it is not so much an ending as it is a re-creation, a new creation. The symmetry of Scripture is breathtaking. In Revelation 21, St. John echoes and informs by God's word what God had given to Isaiah 800 years earlier. In Isaiah 65:17, we read, "Behold I will create new heavens and a new earth. The former things will not be remembered, nor will they come to mind." That new heaven and new earth will be characterized by life for there will be no death there (verse 20). The people of God will live in security and enjoy the fruit of their labor, doing work that is personally fulfilling and enjoying loved ones (verses 21-23). We shall enjoy intimate fellowship and perfect communication with our God (verse 24) and perfect communion with the entire created order. (verse 25).

And John records the vision of God he saw with these words:

Then I saw a new heaven and a new earth, for the first heaven and the first earth were passed away, and there was no longer any sea. I saw the Holy City, the New Jerusalem, coming down out of heaven from God, prepared as a bride beautifully dressed for her husband. And I heard a loud voice from the throne saying, "Now, the dwelling of God is with men, and He will live with them. They will be his people; God himself will be with them and be their God. He will wipe every tear from their eyes. There will be no more death or mourning or crying or pain, for the old order of things has passed away." (Revelation 21:1–4)

Now, there is the purpose of the living Word of God, Jesus, the Messiah, the Son of God. The old order will cease to be filled with the fruit of human sin, death, and its attendant minions.

What God intended from before the beginning will one day be birthed in perfect peace.

He who was seated on the throne said, "I am making everything new!" then He said, "Write this down, for these words are trustworthy and true." He said to me, "It is done. I am Alpha and Omega, the Beginning and the End. To him who is thirsty I will give to drink without cost from the spring of the water of life.'" (Revelation 21:5–6).

Amen, even so come, Lord Jesus. (Revelation 22:20b)

3

God, Spirit, Word (Son)

"In the beginning God created the heavens and the earth. Now the earth was formless and empty, darkness was over the surface of the deep, and the Spirit of God was hovering over the waters. And God said…" (Genesis 1:1-3a).

The Word of God

Now I have added the last three words to the text for our consideration, "And God said." As we begin this reflecting, we must remind ourselves that it is an improper treatment of the Old Testament text to Christianize it without first considering it in its original context and the meaning it would have for the people of God in the Old Testament historical setting. To fast forward for you one moment, I am going to equate "and God said" with the "living Word of God" whom we understand to be Jesus as in the prologue to John's gospel in chapter one. To do so is to Christianize the Hebrew text which I told you we should not do at first. But I need to do this to illustrate my teaching for you.

Genesis 1 describes creation as the action of God complemented by the Spirit hovering over the waters (NIV) followed then by the three words, "And God said." Viewing this from a Hebrew point of view, they had an evident belief in God and belief in the Spirit of God.

The Hebrew Concept of the Word

Then, the ancient Hebrew would have no difficulty with the concept of the Word of God as God's spoken directives to his people usually delivered by his servants, the prophets. In the Old Testament, the concept of the Word of God, first spoken and then written gains dramatic significance with the rise of the classical and writing prophets, particularly Samuel, Elijah, and Elisha. But, of course, the Hebrews would not have a concept of God's Son being an agent in creation. However, this is not to say that they had no concept of God having a son. They did believe (Psalm 2:7f) that in the coronation of their kings, the Lord entered into a father-Son relationship with the king. So, the Hebrews did have a strong theology in the word of the Lord expressed both by kings but particularly by prophets.

The Irrevocable Power of the Spoken Word

To the Hebrew, the power of God's word and then the words of men in blessing and cursing seems to take on a life of its own. Human events were affected by the word and an oath, once made, could not be rescinded. One of the most tragic Old Testament episodes is that of Jephthah and his daughter in Judges 11. Chosen by God to deliver his people the Gileadites from Ammonite oppression, he vowed to God if God would give him victory in battle, he would sacrifice as a burnt offering to God, as thanksgiving, whatever comes out of the door of his house when he returned from battle. Jephthah expected an animal to come out of his house, for in those days, the animals stayed in an enclosure immediately inside the door of their houses. Regrettably so, it was not an animal but his teenage daughter who came out of the house. In time, Jephthah kept his word. That is a quite tragic and negative example of what it meant to the Hebrews to keep their word and how significant God's word was to them as well. Therefore, a word once uttered seemed to have a life of its own either for blessing or cursing.

The Son of God Speaking in Creation

So while we may not imply the presence of the Son of God in the words, "And God said," we may infer the action of the Son when we consider the totality of biblical theology. For without doubt, there is a progression in understanding and in the personification of the word of God or the word of the Lord from Genesis into the New Testament via God's speaking through his servants the prophets, combined with the earlier discussion and the equation of Jesus with the personification of Wisdom in creation in Proverbs 8.

In John's theology, Jesus becomes the Word active in creation through whom all things are made, the agent of life and light. The word *logos* in Greek thought is the logic or reason which brings order and harmony to the universe; to me, this is close to the idea of God's sovereign providence. At any rate, the apostle in the Apocalypse (Revelation), which expresses one of the highest understandings of Jesus Christ in the New Testament, describes the Victorious Christ, the rider on the white horse, in Revelation 19:11–13.

I saw heaven standing open and there before me was white horse, whose rider is called Faithful and True. With justice he judges and makes war. His eyes are like a blazing fire, and on his head are many crowns. He has a name written on Him that no one knows but He Himself. He is dressed in a robe dipped in blood, and his name is the *Word of God*.

Therefore, for me, the witness of biblical theology will permit us to understand "and God said" as the creative work and word of the eternal Son of God.

So present in creating is the Father, Son, and Spirit. God creates by ordering the creation by his word through his Spirit. As we have seen above, bara is always a new work which has never existed before done by God alone. The material God used for creating was nothing. Creation is not a projection of the essence of God; it is not God taking part of his being or essence and giving it to the created order. Creation is God making a new substance and giving it life, first in forming it and secondly in filling the form. For example, day two of creation is the form—

sky and water, and day five of creation is the filling of day two with fish and fowl.

God deliberated. God willed. God spoke. It was done. He willed life—that is the mind and volition of God the father. He commanded and spoke life—that is the action of God the father and God the Son. God the Spirit ordered—subdued chaos and maintains the universe and the creatures in this world for their good and his glory.

Someone remembered an anecdote from Martin Luther's life. Some youths were taunting him about what God did before he created the world. After some deliberative delay, Luther replied that before God created the universe, he was making switches to use on these unruly boys who ask such irreverent questions. Somehow, I doubt that Luther said this, but I do believe that when we affirm that God the Father, Son, and Spirit created the universe, we are asserting this.

1. The presence of God preceded creation.

2. The person of God preceded creation.

3. And the purpose of God preceded creation.

God is—nothing else needs to be said. And God is for you and me; there is no stronger truth. Our God is immersed and in flesh in his world. His purposes are immutable. His love is immeasurable. His grace is undefeatable. His providence is sure and certain. His Word is true.

4

Reflecting on the Chaos

"Now the earth was formless and empty, darkness was over the surface of the deep, and the Spirit of God was hovering over the waters"

(Genesis 1:2).

Having now dealt with Genesis 1:1 and 1:3a, we now move to verse 2. Verses 1:3 through 2:3 will describe the ordering of the heavens and the earth. Why then do we have verse 2 between the general statement about God's having created and the more detailed accounting from verse 3 on expressed in a day by day format?

Part of the answer is that God is taking his creation, including all creation and particularly his image-bearing creature, humankind, to a new heaven and a new earth in the last day (Revelation 21). Since God knows that you and I need redemption, spiritual transformation, before he created the universe (Ephesians 1:4), God also knew that "something" would interrupt the flow, form and function of his world which would necessitate a re-creation. So humankind always lives in a tension between the journey to the new heaven and the new earth and the danger of being pulled back into the "darkness over the surface of the deep."

The Goodness of the Lord

We must express this thinking seriously and carefully. The one axiom which must underlie all our theology is that our Lord is good. He wants what is best for us, and he does everything in his power to work all things for our good. This is the essential meaning of Romans 8:28, "And we know that in all things God works for the good of those who love Him, who have been called according to His purpose." The theology of this verse extends into the past to pre-creation as well as into the future.

God Allows the Chaos before He Orders It

Genesis 1:2 tells us that the Lord God brought forth his creation by ordering it by his word under the direction of his Spirit. We are not to understand that this formless, empty darkness preexisted God, for clearly verse 1 tells us that it is the first creation of God as part of the fabric of the earth. This concept is variously called chaos or primordial chaos or that which existed by God's hand before he created anything else, and it need not at this point be regarded as evil but as simply unordered.

God created this unordered matter and space and time and then by his Spirit, brought order from it as described in the seven days of creation. God ordered the world by his word (And God said) through his Spirit. He does this by giving form to the shapeless, filling the empty, subduing the deep darkness by bringing light and truth and goodness and beauty and grace into being.

Our human experience, from our perspective today, tells us that we cannot escape the realization that there is within our world a fundamental disordering of the universe which wreaks havoc and inflicts pain in the human condition. Our world is temporarily under the control of a menace, an evil which works randomly and selectively at the same time in a strategic crusade against God and his purpose in this world.

Being honest, we must wonder why God permitted this to take place. This primordial chaos is the mayhem in our world; it is the spirit which opposes God. Why did God allow this?

The Integrity of God

Could God have not just as easily spoken his world into being without the chaos? Of course. But there seems to be an essential honesty or integrity in God which does not permit God to take advantage of our situation. Perhaps I can best illustrate this truth in thinking about Jesus. When Jesus came into this world, he had the right to appear as the King of kings and Lord of lords, to make use of his divine attributes, his sovereign omnipotence, and his omniscience. He had every right to rule, but he chose to entrust himself to humankind in the most vulnerable, most precarious form that he could. He came in the form of a little baby whose life and well-being must be placed in human hands.

In his ministry, did he not have the perfect right to use his deity as the source of his power to heal the sick, to feed the hungry, to bring restoration of wholeness to broken lives? Of course, he did. But he chose not to avail himself of heavenly powers legitimately belonging to him. He was self-limiting in his freedom to be and do.

Rather his ability to perform miracles flowed not from his Son-Father relationship as God, but his power flowed from His son-Father relationship as the perfect Adam, the second Adam who lived in this world as Adam could have—as a human being. The capitalized "Son" refers to the eternal Son of God. The small case "son" refers to Jesus as a human being without any advantage over other human beings as they relate to the Lord. Jesus's power flowed from his daily, trusting, prayerful bond with his Father. Jesus came to show us that being faithful, obedient servants of the Lord is certainly a possibility and God's intention for Adam and for you and me. This He believed so strenuously that he gave himself to die for you and me that we might have life with him by the Spirit.

Permitting Evil

Just as Jesus refused privileges that were his right to exercise in his earthly ministry, so God in creation refused privileges that were his right to exercise. Verse 2 of Genesis 1 expresses that

God permitted; that God allowed the possibility of "something" in his world from the outset that opposed Him. This we call evil, and it is represented by the primordial chaos.

Here we must be careful. *I have just said that God allowed the possibility of evil in the primordial chaos. God did not create the primordial chaos as evil, but he did create the atmosphere for it. God created the earth formless, empty and dark which in and of itself is neither good or bad, right or wrong. Having come from God's hand, it simply is. And yet it has the capacity for being "other than God;" that is, other than good and loving for being against God.*

Human Testing

This "other than God" is allowed to exist and to oppose God if it chooses because God does not desire human service, submission, love, and worship which has no choice. God wants us to praise and love him because we want to, not because we must. For that reason, he permits a reservoir of evil to exist. God created humankind with the freedom to choose: serving him or disobeying him.

Our love must be tested. And the Scripture bears witness to this with regularity. The serpent shows up in the garden. Abraham is asked to sacrifice his son. Job is shown to be under the attack of Satan. Jesus faces the desert/wilderness testing to determine what methods he will use in establishing his kingdom in this world.

This possibility for evil is described as formless and shapeless (*tohu*), indicating it is useless and without purpose; it is confused and lacks understanding; it is nothingness.

Secondly, the chaos is described as empty (*bohu*) which indicates desolation; it has no content, no filling, and no hope.

Thirdly, the chaos is dark—what Scripture will later call gloom, terror, and death, the ultimate end of those who oppose the life and light-giving God.

Finally, this darkness has an aspect to it which is described by deep, the "*great tehom*" (Hebrew for the deep). There is a depth to this darkness—a fullness to its emptiness which will become in Scripture the reservoir of evil, and later, the great abyss (Revelation 20:3) which is the eternal home of the devil, the beast, the false prophet, and all who follow in their stead, even death and the grave, the abode of the unredeemed dead.

Personal Evil and Sin

Genesis 1:2 tells us that this chaos exists within the fabric of creation which means, unfortunately, that the chaos exists within your heart and mine. Therefore, all creation is in constant danger of returning to the original chaos, the pandemonium of mayhem. This chaos is the *unholy disorder* which opposes God in his world. It has degenerated into *disorder* from *unordered*.

Unordered is neither good nor evil; disordered expresses the evil in opposition to the goodness of God.

All this being said, in Christ, you and I affirm that our heavenly Father will by his providential, sovereign, loving goodness assert his will and accomplish his purpose in this world for our good as his creatures and for his glory as our creator, redeemer, sustainer.

Sometimes it seems that the world and even the church have lost their bearings and will most certainly crash in certain destruction. But then we remember that despite the formless chaos, the empty voids in our hearts, and the dark patches through which we must walk at times, we remember that the Spirit of God is hovering over the waters of our lives and world. Gently, he moves and works the wonder of his grace.

For the Spirit gently melts, molds, forms, shapes, and fills us. He gives structure to our lives, and by his word, he gives us life. The Spirit prevails over this watery expanse bringing order to chaos as described in the seven days of creation. It is a watery deep, a watery tehom, perhaps meant to be understood as the vast depth of our self-absorptions.

Taming the Watery Chaos

Why does the writer use the term waters? The word for waters is *mayim*. Water is one of the necessary elements for life in our world. It was not available at a spigot or faucet; its procurement involved regular and systematic labor. God provided the rains which were highly valued and celebrated. However, the force which often accompanied water carried a negative connotation, usually that of judgment. In our text, the connotation is neither negative nor positive. It simply is and in God's providence; the Spirit will corral the watery chaos for the good purpose of the Lord.

The water in this text is negatively described in the sense that it seems incomplete and lacking purpose. As water, it has no form; therefore, it is useless and confused. It is empty, which means that it is unaware of any purpose, and it is dark because it does not know light; that is, it is spiritually void. And it is deep because it knows not God and escape from it is possible only by the grace of God in the movement by the Spirit of God to bring order and purpose to it.

This theme of the water's blessing and the water's chaos (which is judgment) will run like a crimson cord throughout the fabric of the Scripture. It is present in the great flood of Genesis 6 when the Lord sends the unrelenting rains bringing judgment on humankind for their arrogance and prideful rebellion against his wondrous gift of grace. Yet the grace is preserved and finds victory because the flood waters give life to Noah and his family in the ark provided by the Lord for those who trust him.

We have already mentioned the Exodus in the "Beginnings" context. The Lord uses the parting of the Red Sea to deliver his people from Egyptian enslavement and at the same time to destroy Pharaoh's army. In Numbers 20, the complaining Israelites demand water which the Lord provides when Moses strikes the rock at Meribah. In grace, the community receives water, but in judgment, Moses and Aaron are not allowed to accompany the nation into the promised land because these two leaders failed to honor God properly.

Next, in Joshua 3, the nation is ready to enter the promised land under the leadership of Joshua, and as they enter into the waters of the Jordan opposite Jericho, the river parts, and they cross on dry ground. This is grace.

In 2 Kings 2, before Elijah is translated into heaven in a whirlwind, he and Elisha cross the Jordan near Jericho on dry ground. Following Elijah's translation (his movement from earth to heaven), Elisha strikes the waters of Jordan with Elijah's cloak, and they part for him as he passes back onto the other side. The first miracle done through Elisha is the purification of the water of Jericho. The Old Testament prophets, chief among them Elijah, regularly bring judgment and blessing on Israel by the withholding of rain bringing drought and the abundance of water bringing life—judgment and grace. For Jonah, the sea is both judgment and blessing.

Moving to the New Testament, Jesus is baptized in the waters of this same Jordan River. On the churning waters of the Sea of Galilee, he will speak his "Peace, be still." Jesus's first miracle recorded by the Apostle John is the changing of water into wine. He offers the Samaritan woman spiritual water which will bring eternal life. Then, in perfect servanthood, during the Last Supper, he stoops to wash the disciples' feet with water. Each and all of these examples demonstrate the continued activity of the Spirit of God in bringing continuing victory over the chaotic waters in our lives. This theme is so significant that in the new creation in Revelation 21:1, when the old order has passed away and the new has come, "there was no longer any more sea."

So the watery expanse which represented the reservoir of disorder and dis-ease in opposition to the plan and purpose of God is eradicated. But the water is still present—preserved and ordered according to God's purpose and operating according to his grace in the river of the water of life (Revelation 22) which flows from the throne of God producing fruit which brings healing to the nations, and the invitation is given by the Spirit and the church in 22:17, "Come! Whoever is thirsty let him or her come; and whoever wishes, let them take the free gift of the water of life."

So why does the Genesis text read in the following way? Why do we have verse 2 inserted?

"In the beginning God created the heavens and the earth. *Now the earth was formless and empty, darkness was over the surface of the deep, and the Spirit of God was hovering over the waters.* And God said, "Let there be...""

We need verse two because the Lord knew that we would need to understand that there exists by his permission a force in this world which has chosen to withstand him and his will. The existence of such a force, spiritually and reflectively speaking, enables us to conceive the interaction of our sovereign Lord in our lives and the permission by him of our human will in our decision-making.

And those of us who desire to follow Christ as Lord and Savior need to expect that we too shall face the onslaught of this force, this evil, which confronts God. On our faith journeys, as Christ did, so do we face the continuing pull of the chaotic mayhem as we seek the kingdom of God in our lives. That is what verse two of this text helps us understand.

5

The Work of the Spirit of God

Now the earth was formless and empty, darkness was over the surface of the deep, and the Spirit of God was hovering over the waters.

The Work of the Spirit before Ordering and Governing

We have looked in some depth at the work of the Eternal Son/Word of God in creation based on the entire biblical witness emphasizing the phrase at the beginning of each day, "And then God said."

Preceding this work of the Son is the work of the Spirit of God who is described in this text as hovering over the waters. Most translations use the word *hovering* as the work of the Spirit. *Hovering* is a word which describes the action of a bird watching over her young. So, the Spirit of God works for good in regard to the churning chaos; that is, he watches over the chaos in terms of governing it as a watery wasteland without, at this point, bringing order to it.

This is an important understanding which we must not miss. Even as chaos, the *tehom* is not a rival to God; it is still created matter and subservient to God's purpose. The Spirit is preparing it for the Word of God which will bring created order to it. One thing that does seem sure is that the work of the Spirit in verse

31

two represents a generalized description of created matter which, beginning in verse three, will yield to the particularization of the spoken word of God as he calls forth the light, the forming of the days, and later the filling of the days.

Spirit, Wind, and Breath of God

An additional note which I like is the understanding that the Hebrew word *ruah* which is translated here as Spirit (of God) is the same word translated sometimes as breath (of God) or wind (of God). I like the translation Spirit of God, but there are some interesting translations which come to the fore when we use breath or wind. For example, Wycliffe renders the phrase, "the Spirit of God was borne upon the waters," connoting for me the comforting idea that the Spirit is totally in control of the chaos before the ordering begins. Sometimes I think in our world, there are those who would take every opportunity to misrepresent the theology of God's sovereignty in the creation and the provident care of his creation. In Wycliffe's version, the idea is conveyed that the watery chaos is the servant of God, the vehicle of God and in no way does the Spirit have difficulty controlling them.

A parallel realization comes when we substitute the word breath in place of Spirit which the Knox Bible has done. "The earth was still an empty waste and darkness hung over the deep; but already, over its water, *stirred the breath of God.*" Here we enjoy the thought that the creation is God-breathed, even in its chaotic state, stirred by the breath of God.

Regarding the "wind" of God rather than Spirit reminds us of Jesus's teaching with Nicodemus in John 3. Jesus tells Nicodemus that no one can see the kingdom of God unless he is born again. The Pharisee takes him literally and asks how one can return to his mother's womb for a second birth. Jesus answers,

I tell you the truth, no one can enter the kingdom of God unless he is born of water and the Spirit. Flesh gives birth to flesh, but the Spirit gives birth to spirit. You should not be surprised at my saying, "You must be born again." The *wind* blows where it pleases. You hear its sound, but you cannot tell where it comes from or where it is going. So it is with everyone born of *the Spirit*. (John 3:5-8)

Thus, Jesus uses wind and Spirit interchangeably in regard to the spiritual birth even as it possible to use wind for Spirit in the creation account.

The Work of the Spirit in Creation and Re-Creation

Enlarging our view of the work of the Spirit of God to include all Scripture, we find these categories.

In addition to the creation of the universe, the *Spirit's work in the Old Testament is the formation, sustenance, and preservation of the people of God.* The Spirit continually comes upon different men or women to prepare them for a particular service such as Moses, Joshua, the Judges, Saul, David, and the prophets.

A third creative action of the Spirit is the birth of Jesus. In Luke 1:35, the angel Gabriel informed Mary, when she asked how she could become pregnant without a husband, "The Holy Spirit will come upon you, and the power of the Most High will overshadow you." St. Matthew records that before Joseph and Mary began to live as husband and wife, "she was found to be with child through the Holy Spirit."

Add to creation personal empowerment and sustenance of the people of God in the Old Testament as the Spirit's work, the incarnation of the eternal Son of God who lives in human flesh, the creation of the church, the new Israel of God, the People of God. In Acts 2, it is by the power of the Holy Spirit that the church is called into existence as a people who trust in Jesus as Savior and Lord. The Spirit descends and fills all in the house, and in 2:17, Peter reminds the gathered ones that Joel promised, "In the last days, God says, I will pour out my Spirit on all peoples."

The Work of the Spirit in Filling

In the Old Testament, the Spirit comes upon individuals to equip them and fill them for a particular service for the Lord. It occurs with Moses and David, the priests and prophets. However, as an example of this filling, I want to share with you about Bezalel.

Very few of us have ever heard of him. In Exodus 31:1-5, we find the Lord's instructions for the building of the tabernacle or the tent of meeting.

Then the Lord said to Moses, "See, I have chosen Bezalel son of Uri, the son of Hur, of the tribe of Judah, and I have *filled him with the Spirit of God*, with skill, ability and knowledge in all kinds of crafts—to make artistic designs for work in gold, silver and bronze, to cut and set stones, to work in wood, and to engage in all kinds of craftsmanship.

I use Bezalel as this example of filling because the people of God sometimes forget that *all work at the behest of God is holy work, and the workmen or women should be Spirit-filled.* Those who serve on building and grounds and finance teams for the church must be filled by the Spirit for the proper performance of their callings just as much as are preachers, teachers, and nurturers of the people of God.

You and I should be filled with the Spirit. Perhaps our names will not be remembered by humankind as Paul or Luther, Augustine or St. Francis, but our lives and contributions to the kingdom are just as significant as anyone else's. We shall have to await the New Testament to have a different understanding of being filled by the Spirit.

The Spirit also is present in Jesus's baptism. Mark 1:10 tells us that at Jesus's baptism, the Spirit descends on him like a dove. And in Luke 4:18, Jesus makes the claim in Scripture that the Spirit of the Lord is on him. It is New Testament theology that when we are called of God to salvation and baptized, that you and I are also gifted by the Spirit for service in Jesus's name as we utilize our giftedness in the building up of the church of God.

The Work of the Spirit with Scripture

Referencing the Knox Bible's translation of Genesis 1:2 above in calling the Spirit the breath of God, my reflecting turns to St. Paul's majestic statement about the Scripture in 2 Timothy 3:16, "All Scripture is God-breathed, and is useful..." Therefore, both the Scripture and the creation are God-breathed making them holy and expressive of the Creator of the universe and the author of the written Word. Ultimately this means that our creation, our lives, are also God-breathed, and we are meant to live in accordance with the God-breathed Word of God.

The Gospel of John presents a magnificent portrait of the Holy Spirit, particularly regarding Scripture. In John 14:16-17, Jesus promises the *Spirit of Truth will guide* the disciples and *be with* them forever, promising that they *will know him*, and that he will *be with them* and will *be in them*.

Note these affirmations. The Holy Spirit is truth; there is no error, no deception, and no confusion in the teaching by the Spirit.

The Spirit guides the church, directs the church in accordance with the church's willingness to seek guidance and wisdom.

Thirdly, the Spirit will be present with the disciples forever (that includes you and me). This means a continuing presence rather than an intermittent presence as in the Old Testament. No longer does the Spirit empower a woman or man for one task or function then withdraw, but since Pentecost, the Spirit indwells God's people continuously.

In John 14:26, Jesus promises that the Spirit will "teach you all things and will remind you of everything I have said to you." This promise directly speaks to the transmission of the Old and New Testament as the God-breathed Word of God.

How were the apostles and their associates able to record what they did, particularly the gospel writers, concerning the life and teachings of Jesus? The Holy Spirit brought these things to their minds.

Lastly, Jesus reiterates that the Spirit will testify about Jesus (John 15:26) and finally in 16:13, the Spirit will guide the disciples into all truth.

The Work of the Spirit in the Life of the Church

"To each one the manifestation of the Spirit is given for the common good." In this verse in 1 Corinthians 12:7, Paul expressly says that the Spirit gives every Christian certain gifts (manifestations) for the common good. The purpose of the gifting of each Christian is for service in the church and in the world so that the church, the body of Christ, may be built up or increased and the kingdom of God advanced in the world. We must remember and reflect that gifting, no matter how wonderful, never serves to bring an individual glamour or adulation. The purpose of God's gifting to us is that we use them to bring glory to God and praise of the Son.

Paul tells us in Romans 5:5 that "God has poured out his love into their hearts by the Holy Spirit, whom He has given us." The most significant Spirit gift which does the most good in human living and glorifies God the greatest is the gift of love or agape.

Note that in 1 Corinthians 12:27–31, Paul names the gifting and offices of the church: apostles, prophets, teachers, workers of miracles, healing, helping others, administrations, and tongues. No one person has all these gifts and in closing, he advises to "eagerly desire the greater gifts. *And now I will show the most excellent way."*

Immediately, following these words, he writes 1 Corinthians 13, the love chapter in which he describes the greatest gift any Christian can have and all Christians must have regardless of any other gifts the Spirit has given them. What he is saying is that this chapter is a snapshot of our lives in Christ: be patient, kind, do not envy. Don't be boastful and proud or rude. Do not be self-seeking, easily angered or keep records of wrongdoing. Don't delight in evil but rejoice with the truth. Always be protective, trusting, hoping without interruption and persevere in the faith (paraphrase of 1 Corinthians 13:4–7). Then in verse eight, he confidently affirms, "Love never fails."

Remember that this passage began in chapter 12 discussing spiritual gifts with Paul insisting in 12:7 that the purpose of the gifts is for building up the body of Christ. Therefore, the most important thing any Christian can do is to learn to love others in the service of Christ. This is what St. Paul means by the ...*most excellent way.*

What does St. Paul mean by love?

Over 95 percent of the time in the New Testament when the English word *love* is translated, standing behind that word is the Greek word *agape*. *Agape* means that one should try to do what is best for everyone *in all circumstances and situations*. When you reflect on that statement, you will find it not to be as easy as it might seem.

At heart, *agape* is living out toward others (and ourselves) the life God is always living toward us and others. The Spirit gives us that gift and enables us to love when loving is hard. Agape is choice love, volitional love whereby we must make conscious decisions to *do what is best* for all people concerned in every situation. That means that love in this sense is not first qualified by affection or by friendship but is defined by goodness. God is always good toward us, and he intends for us to be good toward others and toward ourselves. "Love the Lord your God with all your heart and with all your soul, and with all your mind and with all your strength... love your neighbor as yourself."

Paul has another expression of Christian living found in Galatians 5:22. Paul lists the fruit of the Spirit, the marks of true Christian living: love, joy, peace, patience, kindness, goodness, faithfulness, gentleness, and self-control. All of what John and Paul have said above describe how you and I should live in Christ by the Spirit. And in 1 Peter 1:2, St. Peter sums it up by writing,

To God's elect, strangers in the world, scattered throughout Pontus, Galatia, Cappadocia, Asia and Bithynia, who have been chosen according to the foreknowledge of God the Father, through the sanctifying work of the Spirit, for obedience to Jesus Christ and sprinkling by his blood. (1 Peter 1:1–2)

The work of the Spirit for the church is making the people of God holy.

The Work of the Spirit in Hospitable/Invitational Grace

Lastly, it is the work of the Spirit to complete his loving work by continually offering the grace of God to the people in his world. Moreover, he involves us in that great mission. In Revelation 22:17 we read the great invitation of God: "The Spirit and the bride say, 'Come!' And let him who hears say, 'Come!' whoever is thirsty, let him come; and whoever wishes, let him take the free gift of the water of life." There is not a greater summary of the work of the Spirit in regard to the church than chapter 12 in the *Westminster Confession of Faith* entitled, "Effectual Calling." All who will come to Christ are

effectually called, by his Word and Spirit, out of that state of sin and death, in which they are by nature, to grace and salvation by Jesus Christ; enlightening their minds, spiritually and savingly, to understand the things of God, taking away their heart of stone, and giving unto them an heart of flesh; renewing their wills, and by his almighty power determining them to that which is good; and effectually drawing them to Jesus Christ; yet so as they come most freely, being made willing by his grace.

(Book of Confessions)

That paragraph, fully based on scriptural authority, provides a concise yet complete description of the Spirit's work regarding our salvation. From beginning to end, such grace is the Spirit's domain. The Spirit effectually (effectively) calls us out of the state of sin and death in which we find ourselves by the Word of God. The process which leads to life in Christ includes the following:

1. The enlightening of our minds to the things of God.

2. Melting our hearts of stone which refused the good news of God's grace and replacing them with a receptive spirit.

3. Renewing our wills. The Spirit gives us a desire to turn toward his ways and to seek his purpose. Renewing the will may be the most significant change in the process of salvation because the will of humankind is the center, the core of decision and self.

4. The renewing of the will enables God's almighty power to turn us to things that are good. He creates the longing within us for himself and what he wants for us.

5. Thus, he draws us to Jesus Christ.

6. Yet we come most freely, being made willing by his grace.

In John 6:37, Jesus tells his disciples, "All that the Father gives me will come to me, and whoever comes to me I will never drive away." There is no need for the endless debate we have in some circles today over the doctrine of election. In no time or circumstance has my heavenly Father ever forced me to do one thing against my will. Yet I have sinned and opposed his will for my life many times.

He always receives me when, after wandering, I return to him in repentance and trust. I know I belong to him because I know that he chose me to be in him before the creation of the world—holy and blameless in his sight—that is election.

Now the process of the Spirit's call being made effective in my life which brought me to him is a step-by-step event which I chose also at different times and places in my life. *So the Lord chose me, and I have chosen him in response. I hold to my belief* in election because I know that there is nothing good in my life which has occurred without the miraculous presence and power of the Lord.

Did I give birth to myself? Did I learn that God loves me without my mother telling me so? Did I learn the Scriptures without the teaching of others? Did my heart respond to nothing as I floundered and found my way to God? I think not! With all my heart and will, I believe that I came to faith and trust in Jesus Christ because the Spirit of God has, in every moment of my life, nudged me and directed me, by whatever means or by whomever in my life was significant, to bring me to himself. At each holy juncture, I could have resisted and turned around. But I didn't even though sometimes I stumbled. But having stumbled, the Spirit helped me to regain my balance and walk straight again.

Is this doctrine not illustrated by taking a dog for a walk? Some of you may feel that you take your dog for a walk, and some of you may actually think that your dog takes you for a walk. Here is the point: You begin at a certain point, and you have in mind a point one mile away which will be the halfway terminus of your walk. At that halfway point, you will turn around and retrace your jaunt back to the beginning point. But your dog does not quite see the walk in the same way. As you walk in a straight line, your dog veers off to the left to sniff at a fire hydrant yielding to its obvious attraction. Then he returns to you. A half block farther on, he hears a noise in a neighbor's yard and bounds a few hops into the yard to check out the temptation. Then he returns to you. Next, he comes across a vacant lot grown up with brush. His eye catches a movement in the top of the weeds and off he goes to investigate this mystery. Then he returns to you. You meet another dog walking in the way and, while you walk on, your dog stops to say hello and rub noses. Then he looks up; not seeing you, he looks ahead and catches you walking on ahead. So, he takes gigantic bounds and soon catches up with you.

All the time during this walk, your dog belongs to you. He doesn't always stay right with you, but he is aware of your presence and will soon return to you no matter how far afield he may have strayed. Even when he strayed, he still belonged to you because at some point earlier, you found that dog, whether with a breeder or in a pound, you chose that dog and took him home. He belongs to you and, even if you don't realize it, you belong to him.

In our world, we walk with God, and from time to time, we wander off on jaunts of our own, but we always keep our eyes trained for the Lord, and we always return to him. To me, that is the effectual grace of the Lord in my life. He chose me, and now I have chosen him. Thanks be to God.

6

Reflecting on the Days of Creation

"In the beginning God created the heavens and the earth. Now the earth was formless and empty, darkness was over the surface of the deep, and the Spirit of God was hovering over the waters" (Genesis 1:1-2:3)

The Personal Starting Point

And God said, 'Let there be light,' and there was light"

(Genesis 1:3).

The God who created this world is a person, holy person, a person whose essence is goodness, generosity, and love toward his creation. To say God is a person is to say God cares about you and me. He loves us enough to give us life and to offer himself to us with his gift of life. The life God offers us is Jesus, and his life is the light of men (John 1:4). This light which the third verse describes is not just daylight as verse 4 indicates. Daylight is part of it, but in verse 3, this light is the glory of God, the presence of God in his world. The glory of God is the face of God and is the presence of God, the visible manifestation of the person of the Lord with his people. We cannot experience the presence of the Lord without light. This is light in the spiritual sense of revelation: God revealing himself to us is the amount of understanding (revelation) he gives to us, so the glory of God is associated with the spiritual light. Psalm 104:2 tells us that God "wraps himself in light as with a garment." In Isaiah's great vision of the golden future of the people of God (60:1-3), he writes:

Arise, shine, for you light has come, and the glory of the Lord rises upon you. See, darkness covers the earth and thick darkness is over the peoples, but the Lord rises upon you and his glory appears over you. Nations will come to your light and kings to the brightness of your dawn.

In verses 18–19 of the same chapter, Isaiah continues,

No longer will violence be heard in your land, nor ruin or destruction within your borders, but you will call your walls salvation and your gates praise. The sun will no more be your light by day, nor will the brightness of the moon shine on you, for the Lord will be your everlasting light, and your God will be your glory.

The "light" God called forth in Genesis 1:3 is much more than a physical light alone; it's the light of the world which brings spiritual life to the people of God. Creation as presented in Genesis 1 is illuminating. It conveys the idea that by creation, God is bringing the light of his presence to the universe and particularly, to you and me. To me, this verse includes the physical lighting of the universe, but its primary and foundational truth is that the light of the Lord began to fill his world overcoming and taming and transforming the deep darkness of verse 2—the tehom. This light is the glory or aura of the presence of God.

The Setting of the Text

Let's take an overall look at the setting of this text as well as how it works itself out within the New Testament. Genesis 1:3-2:3 is an obvious response to Genesis 1:1-2 with particular emphasis on verse 2. Verse 2 has introduced us to the evocative terms describing the condition of the earth before God works to bring it into order and function. In the state of the earth before verse 3, it is formless, empty with darkness over the surface of the deep portrayed as a watery mass. So, the creation days of Genesis 1:3 *following will describe to us the process by which God brings light to darkness, ordering to the waters, form to the shapeless, filling to the empty, and taming to the deep and mysterious.*

In other words, God takes control of the uncontrollable. He contains the uncontained. He creates the world he intends to create and thus sets in motion processes which will bring ultimate glory to his name by the providence of his sovereignty acting in history through his chosen people. We need to remember that the creation of the heavens and the earth serve as but a theater stage on which the greatest purposes of God will be enacted: the great drama of the redemption of his people in the saving death and resurrection of his Son and then, finally, all things and all the faithful of God will be brought to their intended purpose in the ReCreation of the new heaven and the new earth.

Creation implies the beginning of all things, and by the mere statement of the term *beginning*, ending is also implied. Now a better way of stating this is not to use the word *ending* but perhaps the word *completion*. The completion of all things will include the end of all that which is anti-God, that which is evil—opposed to God, and that which is sinful in women and men—those in rebellion against God. The completion of all things will also include the perfect restoration of order, beauty, and goodness in God's created order. We are intended for a condition in the presence of the Lord in his new creation where truth and right and agape are the avenues of behavior and communication in his kingdom as he intended life to be from the garden of Eden.

"In the beginning God created the heavens and the earth. Now the earth was formless and empty, darkness was over the surface of the deep, and the Spirit of God was hovering over the waters. And God said, 'Let there be light,' and there was light."

Now verse three stands as a general introduction to the rest of the Bible, really but certainly to the rest of this chapter in the very same way that verse one introduces the entire passage, "In the beginning God created the heavens and the earth."

So, when the great Hebrew priest/poet described the progression of creation, he prefaced it by a general statement.

And God said, "Let there be light, and there was light" permeates the rest of the six days of creation, and it is meant to be applied, I believe, to all creation including spiritual life as well as physical life. It applies to spiritual in the sense that light is illumination and power and force. Spiritually speaking, the Apostle John catches this is his matchless prologue in John 1:1-4.

In the beginning was the Word, and the Word was with God, and the Word was God. He was with God in the beginning. Through Him all things were made; without Him nothing was made that has been made. In Him was life, and that *life was the light* of men.

In dealing with the Bible as a unit, there are many other texts which we could note, but I want us to see the beginning, the middle, and the completion points as we move from Genesis 1:3 to John 1:1–4 to Revelation 21–22. *Genesis describes light as the first work of God which illuminates the universe and its inhabitants both physically and spiritually.* John notes the light of the world is supremely revealed in Jesus, the Son of God. In John 8:12 Jesus said, "I am the light of the world. Whoever follows Me will never walk in darkness but will have the light of life." Then in Revelation, John describes the completion of God's purpose in the new Jerusalem.

I did not see a temple in the city because the Lord God Almighty and the Lamb are its temple. The city does not need the *sun or the moon to shine* on it, for the glory *of God gives it light, and the Lamb is its lamp.* The *nations will walk by its light,* and the kings of the earth will bring their splendor into it. On no day will its gates ever be shut, for *there will be no night there.* The glory and honor of the nations will be brought into it. Nothing impure will ever enter it, nor will anyone who does what is shameful or deceitful, but only those whose names are written in the Lamb's book of life. (Revelation 21:22-27)

Then the angel showed me the river of the water of life, as clear as crystal, flowing from the throne of God and of the Lamb down the middle of the great street of the city. On each side of the river stood the tree of life, bearing twelve crops of fruit, yielding its fruit every month. And the leaves of the tree are for the healing of the nations. No longer will there be any curse. The throne of God and of the Lamb will be in the city, and his servants will serve him. *They will see his face, and his name will be on their foreheads. There will be no more night. They will not need the light of a lamp or the light of the sun, for the Lord God will give them light. And they will reign for ever and ever.* (Revelation 22:1-5)

The Temple and the Body

The "temple" reference in verse 22 is quite significant because Walton points out that the seven days of creation might describe the creation of God's temple. God is overseeing this temple construction and can rest on the seventh day because his temple wherein he may be worshipped is finished. Next, it is the consistent witness of the New Testament writers that the faithful people of God compose the body of Christ. In 1 Corinthians 6:19, Paul urges, "Do you not know that your body is the temple of the Holy Spirit, who is in you, whom you have received from God?" And in 1 Corinthians 12:27, he writes, "Now you are the body of Christ, and each of you is part of it."

So, I am saying that the creation of the universe is understood to be the Lord God building his temple which his people will think of as his dwelling place among them in order to receive their adulation and worship and to communicate to them his truth and love (Genesis). Next, Jesus becomes the temple of which each of us is part (Corinthians and John). Last, note that in Revelation, God and the Lamb are the temple of the new Jerusalem. This is biblical symmetry at its best.

Let There Be Light

In that final, eternal day, note the reconstituting of the intended creation perfectly redeemed, and note that this redeemed creation is the opposite of Genesis 1:2, which is described as the primordial chaos.

First, there is light there, but it is not the light which comes from the sun (Revelation 21:23). This light is the glory of God, and the Lamb is its lamp. Perhaps this means that in the beginning, it is first the presence of God which brings light to this world, and it is particularly revealed and disclosed and seen and known in the redeeming work of the Lamb. At any rate, the great tehom, the deep darkness of Genesis 1:2 has been evicted from that wonderful existence which awaits God's people.

This light, secondly, brings illumination to the culture of the earth for the nations and kings walk by this light and use it to honor God (Revelation 21:24). The formlessness and the emptiness of the chaos is gone, having been filled by the ordering majesty of the glory of God.

Thirdly, in verse 27, this light is cleansing for those once impure, or those who have done what is shameful or deceitful will not enter that city, but those will enter it who have been cleansed by the Lamb and have their names written in his Book of Life.

The Water of Life

Fourth, in Revelation 22, the Genesis 1:2 theme continues but moving from light to water. There is water in that new creation, the water of life which flows from God's throne and of the Lamb. No longer are these waters the watery expanse characterized by darkness and confusion. Just as in Revelation 21:23, the light comes from God and the Lamb, so now this second great stanza (Revelation 22:1-5) of John's re-creation hymn continues, but the theme has now become water. The water of life feeds the river in the middle of the city which nourishes the tree of life. There is *no watery shapeless mass here lacking form and purpose. The water is now a perfect servant of God bringing life and health and healing to the nations.*

As in the "light stanza" *of this hymn, there will be no more night; now in the* "water stanza," *there will be no more curse, no sin; nothing that opposes God.* The reason for this is that we belong to the King, to our God whose face we shall see. There is no murkiness, no deep darkness to hide us from his presence. His name is on our foreheads, which means we belong to him.

Then the great hymn returns to its light theme, and we are reminded that the darkness is over forever, both that which attacked us outwardly and that which infiltrated our hearts and deformed our spirits. The Lord God will be our light.

So, the primordial chaos has been tamed; its influence ended forevermore. Praise be to God. Praise be to the Son. Praise be to the Spirit.

This demonstrates the amazing agreement of Scripture. Much of the emphasis today concerning Scripture is its disunity. This pushing of the theme of disunity is the teaching of those who do not take the text seriously. The Old and New Testaments are meant to stand together and rightly understood, they do.

In summary, at the end of the Scripture and in the middle of Scripture, we find the same emphasis as at the beginning. Light, life, water, chaos starts us on our journey, and at the end, we find the glory, the light, the water recreated by the Lord God with their evil counterparts destroyed or banned from the kingdom existence. You and I will not forever face the pain and tribulations of this life dealing with them by faith alone in our Great Physician; in the final day, we shall find the healing, the peace, the glory, and light of the presence of the Lord forever.

7

Form and Filling

Creating the Form for Creation

God saw that the light was good, and he separated the light from the darkness. God called the light "day," and the darkness he called "night." And there was evening, and there was morning—the first day.

And God said, "Let there be a vault between the waters to separate water from water." So God made the vault and separated the water under the vault from the water above it. And it was so. God called the vault "sky." And there was evening, and there was morning—the second day.

And God said, "Let the water under the sky be gathered to one place, and let dry ground appear." And it was so. God called the dry ground "land," and the gathered waters he called "seas." And God saw that it was good.

Then God said, "Let the land produce vegetation: seed-bearing plants and trees on the land that bear fruit with seed in it, according to their various kinds." And it was so. The land produced vegetation: plants bearing seed according to their kinds and trees bearing fruit with seed in it according to their kinds. And God saw that it was good. And there was evening, and there was morning—the third day. (Genesis 1:4-13)

Theology and Science

This text has proved a difficulty to me over the years from the perspective of scientific inquiry and supposition because I did not know how I might or if I should attempt to wed theology with science. Most theologians expressed long ago that the biblical text tells us the why of creation; it speaks to the meaning of creation in our lives today. The method and process of creation was then left to the scientific community. That works for me to some extent, but it fails me, particularly when science began to declare authoritatively that long-held theory, which had not yet been proven to be true, was indeed fact. Thus, science being the study of the physical and natural world and its phenomena, by observation and experiment, made statements which belonged in the faith theological community. Science cannot observe and thus express the ultimate truth of faith because it is of the heart and spirit rather than of the physical and natural.

Moreover, it must be remembered and affirmed that theology, so-called faith, is not what the modern church has settled for in regard to doctrine. The church, retreating from the battle with the world in regard to science, has bought into the scientific claim that faith is simple belief without any evidence or proof for those positions it holds as truth. Faith is often treated by the church as a long shot in the dark rather than a reasoned, considerate position based on physical and spiritual facts. What one believes about the spiritual world around him or her is based on experiential fact and/or long-standing evidence which is firmly based in the knowledge of the written Word of God.

For example, we have the fact of the creation itself which is scientifically verifiable. It is; it exists; pinch yourself to prove it. The old example of the watch-watchmaker is simple enough. If a watch exists, if we can see it, if we can tell time by it, if we can look at it and depend on it, does it not make sense to believe that behind the watch is a watchmaker?

When science looks at what is—the universe around us including you and me—and gleans from what it sees, that it all started with space and time and matter, everything developing from some initial big bang, would that not be for science a faith assumption? Science can prove the big bang perhaps, but it has no legitimate intellectual right to state that there is no one or nothing behind the big bang. A reasonable, logical person would be hard-pressed not to believe that since there has been a big bang, there must be something or someone who caused that big bang. The components which constitute the big bang must come from someone or something. It is illogical to determine otherwise. So much then for my brief excursion into this debate; let's go the biblical text, for it is my discipline and the purpose of these essays.

8

General Observations about Creation

Communication Is Always Risky

The creation of the universe is one way God communicates himself to you and me. God wants us to know him. It is his heart, his desire, his love. You and I are so significant that he sacrificed of himself to give life to us. In creating you and me, God will give up some of his freedom that we may exercise freedom as well. This will mean that God's world will become clouded with partial murkiness and confusion of purpose. Life will not be what God intended it to be because he shared his freedom with us and because we sacrificed our freedom for a falsely promised independence.

Creation also means that not only does God want us to know him, he wants to know us. Would you not think that God knows us already? It is true that he knows us intimately and completely, and that he is always working to do us good in all things which occur, whether we are in his will for our lives or in rebellion against him. However, there is a knowing which comes from interaction, from daily, momentary fellowship.

For example, the Father knew what Jesus would ultimately do with his life: he would go to the cross to pay for our sins and to bring us to new life through faith in him. But Jesus did not know all this from the beginning of his ministry. Even at the baptism, he did not know what the end of his mission would be. He struggled with this all the way along, and finally, by a maturing relationship with his heavenly Father in constant communion and regular times of habitual prayer, the realization grew that he was in contact with his Father, and that he was fulfilling the mission which brought him to this earth. Even on the last night, Jesus went to Gethsemane agonizing in prayer for another way.

And, of course, the bond was so strong by then that he knew that pleasing his Father was absolutely necessary; that obedience to his will was what he desired completely. Anything less than such submission would have sabotaged their relationship as well as his purpose for coming into this world. Jesus knew the Father, and the Father knew him. Jesus, the itinerant rabbi from Nazareth, did not know all about his Father as a human being nor did he know what his suffering and death would mean—as a man facing the cross. He did not avail himself of divine knowledge as a man any more than you and I would be able to. That is why Jesus had to trust his Father, wanted to trust his Father, even knowing that such trust would bring him clearly to a criminal's death on a Roman cross.

It was only by Jesus's living in a trusting relationship with our heavenly Father that they were able to come to know each other in that personal intimacy which is part of full communication with another person.

There is always a great risk when we try to communicate with anyone, but the one who ran the greatest risk is God in giving himself to us first in creation and then, eventually, in redemption. Adam and Eve rejected the loving grace of the Father in creation. When in the fullness of his providence, he came to earth as one of us in the man Jesus, humankind rejected him and crucified him. Quite often, in following the ways of Jesus, if we turn the other cheek, someone hits us with more force or greater weapons than the back of the hand. Creation tells us that God ran a huge risk in trying to introduce himself to us and in getting to know us.

There may be people in your life whom you have set aside and decided to avoid because of issues between you or because your personalities collide. We should be grateful that our Lord God did not give up on us when we chose to go our own ways and do our own things knowing beyond doubt such living was not in accordance with his will for us.

Creational Grace

Creation is the total grace of a God whose essence is goodness, generosity, and agape. It is total grace in that humankind has no role in bringing about creation. Why did God create the universe? There are those who believe God was lonely and wanted companionship. I reject that thinking. The Father, Son, and Spirit (God) are whole and complete within themselves/ himself/herself. They have perfect communication, perfect communion, perfect purpose, perfect harmony without you and me. Life for God could have been much simpler and more harmonious without his creative action.

Creational Goodness

I believe God created because creation is part of God's essence, his being, his core self. "God is good" is the banner that flies over every page of the Old Testament. "Give thanks to the Lord, for He is good; his love endures forever" (Psalm 107:1). The sentiment of this verse stands as sentinel for our understanding of the God of the Old Testament. God never wanted anything but good for you and me, and those who condemn God as the author of anger and rage who acts in wrath against people simply do not understand biblical theology and teaching. They often blame the Lord for events in their lives which he never intended and which they brought about by their own foolish freedom of choice. It is always easier to blame God than take personal responsibility for ourselves. God always wants good for us. Goodness is the permanent condition of the heart of God who has determined without fail to do the best for everyone in every situation.

Creational Generosity

A second part of God's nature is his generosity. Creation demonstrates that what God has, God shares. He withholds from you and me nothing that is good for us. In the garden with Eve, it is the serpent's insinuation that God was holding out on Adam and Eve (Genesis 3:1-5), and that in eating from the tree of the knowledge of good and evil, they would become like God. The serpent argued that God wanted to withhold himself from them.

Creation is the second greatest act of generosity from God to us; the first being, choosing us from before the creation of the world to be adopted as his daughters and sons (Ephesians 1:3-4). God grants us his generosity in giving us life, breath, talents, bodies, and spirits which we may use for his glory. Perhaps his greatest gift of generosity is to permit us the freedom to disagree with him, to rebel against him, to go our own way. That is a strained generosity, for the giver knows what painful costs will accrue to his children when he lets them go their own way, but God will not rescind his generosity to stop us if we want to move away.

Creational Love

The third creational grace is love. Goodness is God's determination to do what is best for us. Generosity is God's preparation of all things good for us to provide and protect us whatever our need. The goodness of God represents his will, his choice, his volition. To say it in human terms, goodness in God's being comes from the will.

Generosity comes from God's heart, his emotions, his desires for us, and love is God's goodness and generosity acting for the good of humankind and the benefit of the universe.

Old Testament Covenant Love

The Old Testament word for God's acting love is *hesed*. Hesed is God's relational caring, his steadfast faithfulness, his covenant vow. It represents the heart of kindness in family relationships and friendships. This is the kind of love David and Jonathan felt and practiced for one another. It is to say it best the committed love of a marriage relationship. God thinks of himself in the Old Testament as the bridegroom of Israel and of Israel as his bride.

He is totally committed to Israel, but Israel strays from him and becomes unfaithful. But the hesed love of God does not forsake Israel but seeks her, waits for her, longs for her, and he always does for her what is best given the circumstances.

New Testament Covenant Love

The New Testament word for love used more than 95 percent of the time is *agape*. Agape is God's love acting for his people, whether they are faithful or rebellious and sinful. This *hesed* and *agape* are not dependent on the one who is loved but on the one who is loving. Agape love is the hands and feet of God's goodness of will and generosity of heart. Agape seeks to do what is best for everyone in every situation. So, God's love applies his goodness and generosity in our lives. "We know that *in all things God works for the good* of those who love Him, who have been called according to His purpose" (Romans 8:28). The italicized section of the preceding sentence is the definition of God's love.

These three, goodness, generosity, and love are God's creational grace toward us and, not incidentally, they are our mission in this world to others as servants of Jesus Christ.

9

Creation by the Word of the Lord

Old Testament

The first phrase in the account of the days of creation is "And God said." In any general reading of the Old Testament, one must notice the repeated uses of the phrase, "And God said." Most often, the phrase is, "The Word of the Lord," but there are others such as "The Word of God." God speaks to the people in his world. He spoke to Adam and Eve, Noah, Abraham, the patriarchs, Moses, Joshua, Samuel, David, and the prophets. God spoke to Sarah, Hagar, Miriam, Deborah, Hannah, Huldah the prophetess and did mighty works through Naomi and Ruth in the preparation for the birth of David. He preserved the Davidic dynasty through Jebosheba who saved Joash, the baby prince from the hands of his evil grandmother Athaliah. Esther is instrumental in saving the people of God from the Persians. There is no gender imbalance in the mighty workings of God.

New Testament

In the fullness of time, he spoke most eloquently, truthfully, and lovingly in his personal and living Word, his son Jesus. Following Jesus, God speaks to us through the apostles who personally knew Jesus (Peter, James, John, Matthew, Jude) and through associates of the apostles (Mark, Luke, Paul) and, in time, gave us the New Testament through them.

It is by his Word that God has communicated himself and his Purpose to us. The written Word of God is his revealed will to his people by the Spirit of God. The New Testament is the supreme revelation of God's will, and on these documents are based the creeds and confessions, the thinking and preaching of the apostolic fathers, the preachers and teachers of former generations. But note the teaching of all others must be based on the Scripture as its primary source.

Interpreting Scripture

Having said this, we must also say that God's Word may also be interpreted to us by human experience, church traditions, and human reason, but these must be in agreement with the written Word by cultural considerations which are tested in agreement with the written Word and by human reason. It is by these standards based on the Scriptures that Christian life and thought must be ordered. This means that the Holy Spirit is able continually to inform the church of scriptural truth and interpretation to which former generations were ignorant perhaps for cultural reasons.

So, the interpretation of the Scripture is not relegated just to what those in the past have said, perhaps the far distant past. Is the Spirit of God dead and no longer working in his people? Of course not. As my reformed communion affirms but does not always practice, the church must always be open to the reformation of herself in doctrine and practice. And how is this to be done without falling into error? It must be done "according to the Word of God and the call of the Spirit."

In other words, as Christ's followers, we shall not come across scriptural interpretations or human experiences or cultural reasoning which we may consider appropriate for accepted belief and conduct, *unless we find them in agreement with the Word of God and the call of the Spirit.*

Simply summarized, neither the Spirit of God nor human experience or reason or any other teaching found can be considered authoritative if it is in conflict with the teaching revelation of Holy Scripture.

The Transmission of the Word

God's word in creation has continued throughout the centuries by his sovereign providence. First, he spoke through the created order, and humankind may still be aware of the person and presence of God in the universe, but such material awareness alone does not serve to bring us to Christ. That requires a more personal and certain word. Next, he caused the recording of his word in the books of the Old Testament. Then he spoke by the living Word, his son Jesus. Jesus, wholly human and wholly divine, came to live among us speaking the truth and love of God's voice already spoken in the Old Testament and fulfilling God's promises entirely in himself. He became and fulfilled in his life and death the covenant love of the Father—the *hesed*, the steadfast, faithful, and committed love to us which nothing can break; by his death and resurrection, he offers to us the elegant freedom of new life, forgiveness for sin, and empowered by the Spirit to become holy.

Inspiration of Scripture

God speaks to us in the written Word comprised of the Old and New Testaments. Paul writes in 2 Timothy 3:16, "All Scripture [the Old Testament in Paul's first century Jewish world] is God-breathed and is useful for teaching, rebuking, correcting and training in righteousness, so that the man [people] of God may be thoroughly equipped for every good work." The Scripture is inspired by God, authoritative for us regarding salvation and Christian living.

Modes of Inspiration Based on Scripture

Fourth, God speaks to us through godly preachers. Preaching is the proclaimed Word of God. For preaching to qualify as the spoken Word of God, it must be scripturally based and inspired by the Spirit. A woman or man who would proclaim the good news of God's love or a word of instruction to others bears a heavy responsibility under God to be faithful in their calling.

Additionally, the Word of God is proclaimed in the sacraments of baptism and the Lord's Supper. In the institution of the sacraments, one sees as well as hears the Word of God presented in drama. In some sense, God's perfect creation becomes sacramental for to God what his Word brought forth was holy and perfect and an instrument of his grace. That is what sacramental means. A sacrament is a God-given grace gift which may bring grace to those outside of Christ or may certainly mark one as having received grace through faith in Christ.

The Significance of Speaking Creation into Existence

Said precedes sight (seeing what God created). Why does "the word" precede the seeing? I believe this to be an important question to which I may not have an adequate answer. Perhaps it will entice you to reflect as well. Before the creation of the universe, seeable things, look around you at the earth, sky, yourself, and others; before the seeable comes into being, God is. God is complete. God is person. God is personal. God is holy person—all of which means that God has already been self-speaking or self-communicating. With whom? With the Trinity. Communication existed within the Godhead. What form does the communication takes? I don't know. But in human terms, God is thinking, purposing, willing, and speaking.'

Hearing God Rather Than Seeing God

I believe the Word of God, the hearing of what God says, is more significant than seeing God, biblically speaking. The second commandment or as I called it earlier in this treatise, the second word reminds us of God's cardinal admonition, "You shall not make for yourself an idol in the form of anything in heaven above or on the earth beneath or in the waters below" (Exodus 20:4)

Why is this one of Israel's cardinal principles? Is it not because all the other nations around Israel worshipped gods which they could see? The Israelites rebelled against the Lord while Moses was on the mountain with the Lord receiving these ten words. In their rebellion, they take all the jewelry, gold, and precious metals which the Egyptians gave them upon exiting Egypt and melt them down... fashioning what from them? They form a golden calf which they worshipped. This is sight worship, idol worship. The Lord would never permit this for his chosen people. Why a calf? The rebellious ones fashioned a calf because it was one of the idol gods of Egypt. Sight worship of an idol seeks to make a deity of created matter. There can be no other source from which to make an idol except created matter because the idol itself is the work of human hands. It is a statue or representation in sight form, seeking to make a physical/material representation of a god.

Now if a "god," an idol, is one who is Spirit being, beyond human sight, how foolish is it to worship a physical representation of a spiritual being? That humanly created "idol god" cannot be seen but can only be experienced by sight. To worship the earth, the sky, the sea, the wind, the rain, the drought is to miss the point of a god.

One's God—the only God—is the unseeable one. Any worship of a physical representation (calf) of a god is, at the most, a worship of some part of the created order. This answers the question of why God speaks; why God uses words to communicate with his people. Our God, the *only* God, does not want us to seek something we can see which represents him. Why? Simply because it is so very easy to slip into the sin of idolatry. In this instance, it becomes easy to worship the seeable object of God rather than God himself. Speaking and hearing, revealing and understanding are more difficult, but ultimately, they are the way of faith and trust.

The Lord always wants us to hear the word and live by the word rather than see the results. In the healings of Jesus (Mark 3:1-6), the sequence almost always follows this order: first, Jesus speaks the word of command to the man with a shriveled hand: "Stretch forth your hand." There is speaking, hearing, and healing. "He stretched it out, and his hand was completely restored." There is the obedience and hearing and faith. The healing is spoken (as God speaks creation) —that is, the healing word is heard by the man in need; then, the healing is seen by the man in need and by all in the synagogue.

This is a significant principle upon which we must reflect. We hear the divine voice before we see the divine action.

Jesus told the masses around him and the Pharisees that they were always looking for signs. "Unless you people see miraculous signs and wonders, you will never believe" (John 4:48). Belief or trust or speaking and hearing always precede sight. Yet we live in a world which demands sight. God's way is word first then belief then proof or sight.

God Speaks Your Language

God discloses himself in creation by his word. "And God said" is verbal communication. He condescends to us in order for us to understand. What if God wanted to tell you something, but you could not understand the language he was speaking? You would become frustrated, and God's efforts would be futile.

Without doubt, for all of us, God spoke plainly and openly. He communicated perfectly his will and purpose for Adam and Eve. There was no communication gap here. They understood. They merely chose to go their own ways.

Diverse National Groups Hear the Proclamation of Jesus in their Native Languages

In Acts 2, we find the story of the founding of the church by the descent of the Holy Spirit on the day of Pentecost. This is as much a creational moment as is Genesis 1. First, there is the form. The disciples are all together in one place. This is followed by the filling. They *hear* a sound which fills the house where they were sitting. The wind is the presence of the Spirit of God, and they *see* tongues (*glossa*) of fire which are the judging and cleansing power of God on the people preparing them for mission. Then the men and women were filled with the Holy Spirit and began to speak in other tongues according to the gift of the Spirit.

Please note now the sequence: gathering (of one mind and purpose), hearing and feeling wind (the coming of the Spirit), seeing the tongues of fire (cleansing as preparation for mission), then they are filled according to the Spirit. The cleansing (tongues of fire) and filling enables them to *speak* (tongues) to the assembled crowd of Diaspora Jews from all over the known world; sixteen nations are named. (Diaspora Jews are those who remained faithful to Yahweh during the dispersion of their forefathers 750 years earlier at the hands of the Assyrians.)

In God's perfect providence, he has now reassembled the descendants of those dispersed faithful believers three quarters of a millennium earlier, precisely at this Pentecost, the first one following the Passover celebration where one Jesus of Nazareth had been crucified and now, as his followers claimed, resurrected from the dead. These three thousand converts will return to their respective homelands and there distribute the message of God's love in Jesus the Messiah.

The apostolic band (it may include the women and family of Jesus mentioned in Acts 1:15) now begins to preach (*glossa*) the love of Christ. That is precisely how God's magnificent love operates in sovereign providence for his glory in the world. As for the tongues which the apostles spoke, they are human languages represented by the Diaspora Jews from all over the known world mentioned above. These languages are not to be confused with the unknown tongue mentioned in 1 Corinthians. That gift of tongues is a praise language used personal devotions. The purpose of the tongues in Acts is for the purpose of evangelization.

The Word of God Spoken by the Spirit

Moreover, the miracle may not be that Peter and the apostles preached in other languages but that the Diaspora Jews heard them in their native languages. The language of the Spirit is a precisely perfect language wonderfully matched for us to speak to others of Christ's love. What does the Spirit wish for us to proclaim? He wants us to speak of Jesus Christ, not societal causes, not a particular church, not a set of doctrines; the Spirit prepares us to speak of Jesus Christ. And the substance of this message about Jesus is not what we have been taught, but what we know about him ourselves, how we have experienced him in our lives. As the Apostle John wrote in the first chapter of his first letter, "We proclaim him who was from the beginning, which we have *heard*, [*hearing comes first*], which we have seen with our own eyes, which we have looked at; and our hands have touched—this we proclaim concerning the Word of Life." Jesus is our message; doctrine and societal issues follow.

The Spirit's Language Is Individualized

The language of the Word of God is sensitive to the needs of the listener. It is sensitive to the level of understanding the listener has. Remember, this is how the Lord speaks to us in creation, in redemption, in our everyday lives. Once we become obedient and willingly speak to others, the Spirit then clearly enunciates this message from our heart to the listener's heart. It is, indeed, a heart language intimately and minutely fashioned just for them. There is nothing generic in this language. It is intimately personal.

Lastly, the Word of God is so personal that the Diaspora crowd marvels at the preaching they are hearing. In verse 7 of Acts 2, they question, "Are not all these men who are speaking Galileans? Then how is it that each of us hears them in his own native language?" The Greek word for *native language* is really one word: it is *dialect*. It is not just a native language but their own idiom—their peculiar accents, we might say. Just as we might recognize a Boston brogue or a Southern twang or a Creole inflection, the Spirit perfectly tailored the apostles' preaching to each individual heart and mind.

And, ultimately, *this explains for me why hearing God is far more momentous than seeing God.* God speaks his creation to us and for us. Indeed, God sings his world into being. Creation is God's wondrous song of grace, mercy, love, and redemption for our good and his glory. May it be ever thus in the living of our lives.

10

Matter, Space, Time and Grace

Creation tells us that all time, all space and all matter are created by God and have been hallowed by Jesus Christ (*Book of Order*, PCUSA, Worship 1.3000). The universe (matter) was created by God, and God made that matter holy by sending his Son, Jesus Christ, as the Word of God made flesh. Therefore, all matter will one day be redeemed to its pristine purpose in bringing honor and glory to God.

Geography of Grace

Space is the arena in which we live and breathe the abode of matter. Though we may worship God at any time and place, God has set aside particular spaces where his worship is expected and is most appropriate. In the Old Testament, there are what the Celtics call "thin places" or locations where God and people met, where lives were transformed and directions given for life.

For example, Abraham's favorite place was the oaks of Mamre at Hebron where he built an altar to the Lord (Genesis 13:18). It was his private worship space. Later instances for worship are Jacob at Bethel and Peniel (Genesis 28 and 32) where he exclaimed, "I have seen God face-to-face."

Better known for corporate worship is the tent of the tabernacle and the Solomonic temple, and for the New Testament, the Herodian temple where Jesus taught and the disciples met on the day of Pentecost when the Holy Spirit descended upon them preparing them for future ministry.

All these places where God and men met are now perfectly completed in the body of Christ of which each of us in him are parts (1 Corinthians 12:27). And then, as you will see below, in the new Jerusalem, we shall have no need of worship space, for the Lord God almighty and the Lamb are the temple (See discussion below).

Creation of History

Creation also brings about the existence of time. On day four, the sun and moon are placed in the sky to separate day from night, to serve as signs to mark sacred times, days, and years. This is the creation of the great clocks of God by which time is measured. Though my science is limited, these concepts recognize behind the changes they note, the rotation of the earth and its revolutions around the sun. Now the ancient Hebrews did not know this, but they observed its consequences. Time and space and matter are especially significant, for this tells us that our lives, given to us in creation by the grace of God, are holy and sacred to him. He loves creation; he does not despise or denigrate it as some do. Particularly, when the fullness of time had come (Galatians 4:4), God sent his Son, born of a woman, at a particular time and space and of matter and spirit to redeem us. God "holy-izes" all matter, space, and time, for in his new creation, we shall enjoy the fullness of our freedoms by being unlimited by any of these components of the material universe.

11

The Filling of Creation

And God said, "Let there be lights in the vault of the sky to separate the day from the night, and let them serve as signs to mark sacred times, and days and years, and let them be lights in the vault of the sky to give light on the earth." And it was so. God made two great lights—the greater light to govern the day and the lesser light to govern the night. He also made the stars. God set them in the vault of the sky to give light on the earth, to govern the day and the night, and to separate light from darkness. And God saw that it was good. And there was evening, and there was morning—the fourth day.

And God said, "Let the water teem with living creatures, and let birds fly above the earth across the vault of the sky." So God created the great creatures of the sea and every living thing with which the water teems and that moves about in it, according to their kinds, and every winged bird according to its kind. And God saw that it was good. God blessed them and said, "Be fruitful and increase in number and fill the water in the seas, and let the birds increase on the earth." And there was evening, and there was morning—the fifth day.

And God said, "Let the land produce living creatures according to their kinds: the livestock, the creatures that move along the ground, and the wild animals, each according to its kind." And it was so. God made the wild animals according to their kinds, the livestock according to their kinds, and all the creatures that move along the ground according to their kinds. And God saw that it was good. (Genesis 1:14-25)

Form and Filling Theme

We are indebted for the following table to W.H. Griffith Thomas in his *Genesis, a Devotional Commentary*, 1946. As you know from above, I have broken out verse three from day 1 as a stand-alone verse indicating the "let there be light" as the light of God's presence, his power and person over all creation. However, picking up at verse 4, we find this superb biblical theme.

Form needs to be over days 123 and Filling needs to be over days 456.

Day 1: Light and Dark

Day 2: Sea and Sky

Day 3: Fertile Earth

1644 Day 4: Lights of Day and Night

1645 Day 5: Creatures of Water/Air

1646 Day 6: Creatures of the Land

Form and filling indicate the work of a master craftsman. The sun, moon, and stars of day 4 fill the day and night of day 1. The sea and sky creatures of day 5 become the inhabitants of the space of day 2, and the land animals of day 6, including humankind, become the tenants of a fertile earth created on day 3. The wonderful realization which Thomas has brought to us in regard to creation plays a very significant theological and biblical role. The Lord makes the human body and fills it with his image and spirit. The universe is formed and filled with people and creatures.

The universe is then filled by the people of God in Genesis 12— Abraham and his family whose distinguishing mark is trusting Yahweh and responding to his call. Such a faith response, believing God's word, results in God's declaring Abraham righteous; that is, walking with God in fellowship and relationship. Abraham, representing a new community of God-persons in the world, receives the filling of Yahweh's love and commitment, his promise, and blessing. Because of the Lord's grace, he promised to Abraham in Genesis 12:

"I will make you into a great nation and I will bless you;"

(He and Sarah are childless.)

"I will make your name great, and you will be blessing."

(He is a nobody from nowhere. That is, he has no standing in the world. And the purpose of this family of faith is to share that faith with all other earthly families.)

"I will bless those who bless you, and whoever curses you I will curse; and all peoples on earth will be blessed through you."

(The earth is now filled with faith and grace which, in time and history, will bring about the blessing of all peoples in the particular blessing of one people to bring glory to God.)

God's "Bara" Revisited

Creation also demonstrates the importance of "living" creatures. On the fifth day in verse 21, bara reappears from verse 1. God's one of a kind, new creation by word, resurfaces with the creation of sea animals, reptiles, and sky creatures. The text describes these creatures as *living* (Hebrew *nephesh*) indicating the presence of the life force with an awareness of self and others that differs from the standard of life shared with plants and trees. God blesses these creatures with a selective share of creativity. They are able to reproduce, and such shared creativity is God's blessing for them. However, their self-awareness will not equal the consciousness of humankind. It is a limited awareness, yet they share in the creativity of God in reproduction of their species.

12

The Creation of Humankind

Then God said, "Let us make mankind in our image, in our likeness, so that they may rule over the fish in the sea and the birds in the sky, over the livestock and all the wild animals, and over all the creatures that move along the ground." So, God created mankind in his own image, in the image of God he created them; male and female he created them. God blessed them and said to them, "Be fruitful and increase in number; fill the earth and subdue it. Rule over the fish in the sea and the birds in the sky and over every living creature that moves on the ground."

Then God said, "I give you every seed-bearing plant on the face of the whole earth and every tree that has fruit with seed in it. They will be yours for food. And to all the beasts of the earth and all the birds in the sky and all the creatures that move along the ground—everything that has the breath of life in it—I give every green plant for food." And it was so. (Genesis 1:26-31)

Humankind and Animals

Five classifications of animal life are detailed in verse 26 of this text: fish, birds, livestock, wild animals or beasts, and creepy crawlies. The creeping things are the lizards, rodents, and insects. Let us note that the animal life and human life is created on the same day, so the text is telling us that we share certain physical traits with animals, and later on in verse 27, certain intellectual, emotional, psychological, and spiritual traits are not given to the animals.

The Wild Animals and Chaos

A second but more significant point for me is the mention of the wild animals, untamed animals or beasts. Whatever biblical version is used, they are the same creatures. They would be the wild game which, in time, following the flood may be used for food. But the wild animals, I believe, also represent in the animal world the residue of that which is *opposed to God as part of the tehom or the great deep* of Genesis 1:2. There seems to be that repository of evil in the universe which is unresponsive to God's authority and which rebels against his goodness.

The second mention of wild animals is in Genesis 3:1. "Now the serpent was more crafty than any of the wild animals the Lord God had made. He said to the woman..." So the literary movement from chapter 1 picks up again in chapter 3. As the Spirit of God brought creative order, grace, peace, and functionality to the deep chaos, we might expect no more chaos. But, in the serpent, the deep chaos persists still.

The clue for interpreting "wild animals" in this way is found in the Genesis 3:1. The serpent is a wild animal and the most crafty—the most cunning and devious of all the wild animals. The presentation of the serpent in this verse as the representative of the untamed world opposed to God sets the biblical stage for a continuing theme in Scripture. This battle which was enjoined in the garden of Eden in Genesis 3 will climax in the ministry of Jesus facing Satan in the wilderness testing following his baptism and, ultimately, on the cross in his death. The Satan Jesus faced is the same serpent/Satan Eve faced in the garden.

Note how the theme develops in Scripture. In Israel's wilderness wanderings, the people are not allowed to eat the flesh of wild animals which have been killed.

Secondly, Job's friend Eliphaz the Temanite looks to a time when a blessed man will "laugh at destruction and famine and need not fear the beasts of the earth. For you will have a covenant with the stones of the field, *and the wild animals will be at peace with you*" (Job 5:22-23).

To Isaiah, the Lord says,

Forget the former things; do not dwell on the past. See I am doing a new thing! Now it springs up; do you not perceive it? I am making a way in the desert and streams in the wasteland. The wild animals honor Me, the jackals and the owls, because I provide water in the desert and streams in the wasteland. (Isaiah 43:18-20)

Ezekiel speaks of the security of that final restorative day for the people of God, "They will no longer be plundered by the nations *nor will wild animals devour them*" (Ezekiel 34:28). Perhaps by now, we have learned that Revelation is never far removed from the rest of Scripture. In the opening of the seals which disclose the biblical understanding of John's interpretation of the human condition, the wild beasts along with famine, plague, and sword are the instruments whereby a fourth of the earth is killed (Revelation 6:8). So clearly, the wild animals are seen as untamed instruments in the arsenal of the weapons of sin and evil.

Jesus and the Wild Animals

However, the most significant mention of wild animals occurs in Mark 1:12 with the testing of Jesus following his baptism. "At once the Spirit sent [drove] him out into the desert, and he was in the desert forty days, being tempted by Satan. He was with the wild animals and angels attended him." As far as the biblical literature is concerned, taking this theme from beginning to end, Jesus's testing in the wilderness is nothing less than his descent into the deep darkness (Genesis 1:2) to confront evil and to defeat it. He is driven by the Spirit into the wilderness immediately following the high moment of self-identification with the Lord and his people in baptism. The wilderness or desert is the Satanic realm, yet this arena belongs to the Father too just as much as the waters of the Jordan, and though Satan may rule it now for a time, the Son has come to take it back and reclaim this desert for the Father's use.

By Jesus's rejection of Satanic testing in the desert, his death on the cross and his resurrection, the evil one is dealt a death blow. As is usual, the Scripture wraps up this theme in Revelation. In Revelation 12:9, the Apostle John pictures the great war in heaven when Satan is cast down to the earth. He depicts Satan in this way: "The great dragon was hurled down—that ancient serpent called the devil, or Satan who leads the whole world astray."

So first of all is the identification of Satan and serpent. Secondly, in Revelation 20:9-10, the armies of the earth surround the camp of the people of God, but fire from heaven defeats and devours them. "And the devil, who deceived them, was thrown into the lake of burning sulfur, where the beast and the false prophet had been thrown. They will be tormented day and night forever and ever." In God's final day, evil and sin will be contained and controlled forever, and death will trouble us no more.

In reflecting, do you ever feel that there is a certain part of you which is untamed, which rebels against the good and right or the better and best? We need not be immoral or depraved or dissolute to partake of the wild animal in each of us. Sometimes we just don't do the best we can, or we know better but do something anyway. Perhaps we love gossip and delight in hurting others. The sharp tongue and the jealous spirit may be as untamed as any wild animal and bring a similar amount of hurt and pain to others. One day, such struggle and trial, temptation and testing will no longer challenge us, and we shall dwell secure beside the river of the water of life near the throne of God and the Lamb.

The Sanctity of Life

Creation establishes the fundamental sanctity of all life with particular emphasis on human life. The creation of humankind is portrayed as the pinnacle of God's work. His great gift of himself in the gift of light as illumination in truth and beauty and goodness is now *reflected* or imaged in humankind. One cannot read these verses without gaining a feel for the satisfaction of God in doing his work of creating his world.

One of the indications of this satisfaction is the sevenfold repetition of the judgment of God, "And God saw that it was good," and on the sixth day in verse 31, "God saw all that he had made, and it was very good." For the creation to be good is for the creation to be an intended expression of the creator's goodness. God's essence is goodness, and so his work of creation is also good. To me, God's goodness means that he intentionally wills that which is pleasing and desirable. This is his will for you and me, for his universe, for all his created order. And even for those who despise or reject him and his ways, he still does good for them given the restrictions which their rebellious ways place upon the Lord.

The basic gift of God's creation is life. Life is sacred and holy to God, including all life of every kind and form. However, human life enjoys a ranking above all other life. In Genesis 9:4f we read,

And for your lifeblood, I will surely demand an accounting. I will demand an accounting from every animal. And from each man too, I will demand an accounting for the life of his fellow man. Whoever sheds the blood of man, by man shall his blood be shed; for in the image of God has God made man.

This passage establishes human government's basic purpose and institutes the foundational principle. Life must be honored to the extent that when a life is taken by one person, the one who takes a life must pay a price: his own life. And the reasoning behind this is each human life is created in the image of God.

We live in a vile and depraved world wherein human life is devalued. Men murder without provocation, almost recreationally by gangs. As of 2018, more than sixty million lives have been sacrificed on the altar of convenience by abortion since 1973. That is in America alone. The enslavement of Africans from an earlier age and the wholesale abortion of millions are a blight on the American dream. We have permitted the establishment of the denigration of human life which cuts across the grain of the holiness and sanctity of life created by God in the beginning.

The Deliberation of God "Then God Said…"

Then God said, "Let us make mankind in our image, in our likeness, so that they may rule over the fish in the sea and the birds in the sky, over the livestock and all the wild animals, and over all the creatures that move along the ground

So, God created mankind in his own image, in the image of God he created them; male and female he created them. God blessed them and said to them, "Be fruitful and increase in number; fill the earth and subdue it. Rule over the fish in the sea and the birds in the sky and over every living creature that moves on the ground."

Then God said, "I give you every seed-bearing plant on the face of the whole earth and every tree that has fruit with seed in it. They will be yours for food. And to all the beasts of the earth and all the birds in the sky and all the creatures that move along the ground—everything that has the breath of life in it—I give every green plant for food." And it was so. (Genesis 1:26-30)

Preceding the creation of humankind in verse 26, the text reads, "Then God said." Before creating us in his image, *God deliberates. That is what the word then indicates.*

God considers, thinks, ponders, and determines which means that you and I do not receive the gift of life from God as an afterthought or just the next act in a series of progressive movements. "Then" indicates that in God's sight, our lives have purpose and meaning; our births are planned, and we are blessed with God's intentionality.

It is a superb gift of the grace of God to be intended. We know we are intended because we were chosen in Christ before the foundation of the world. God chose us which means that God intends us to be and to do his will in our lives for his glory. There is no person more lost than the one who has no sense of belonging and no sense of purpose. The intentionality of the Lord gives us both physical and spiritual life in his image and for his glory. We need a sense of belonging to anchor us in Christ and with others who follow him. This anchoring may be described as peace and security, the assurance that we have a Father and a home. And the sense of purpose we receive from our being chosen applies to our future as belonging does to our past.

In human terms, we take pleasure in being chosen for marriage by our beloved. Someone chose us. They love us. They want to be with us. They long to share time and make history and grow old together. One of the most powerful experiences in life is to realize that our parents chose to conceive us, wanted us, and made us by God's blessing.

Biblically, a third expression of intentionality is adoption. Sometimes adoption brings a stronger reality of being chosen than a natural child. Our adoptive parents made a choice for us. They could have chosen someone else perhaps, but they chose us. When we participate in the intentionality of marriage, birth, and adoption, we are indeed demonstrating the image of our Father within us.

After all, St. Paul reminds us in Ephesians 1:4-6 of the significance of adoption in every Christian's life:

For he chose us in him before the foundation of the world to be holy and blameless in his sight. In love he predestined us to be adopted as his sons through Jesus Christ, in accordance with his pleasure and will—to the praise of his glorious grace, which he has freely given us in the one he loves.

The Primary Filling in His Image

However, following the forming and filling of the tehom with the ordered universe, the foremost filling is that of God in humankind. God makes humankind, male and female, and fills them with his image. The long-standing, quick answer to the meaning of the image of God within us is that we have a measure of free will. God gave us the freedom to make choices about our lives. Animals do not have such freedom in as great a measure. But there is more than free will to what is involved in the image.

To be made in God's image means that we have the ability to reason. In our freedom, we may plan and prepare and perform and complete. Image also means that we are moral creatures charged with the responsibility to determine and make choices. To be moral necessarily implies that humans have conscience which provides us with the knowledge of right and wrong. Such knowledge of right and wrong brings us to choices. And with choices, of course, comes the corresponding consequences. Just as God makes choices, so we may make choices, but when we make wrong choices as God never does, we must then deal with the results of wrong decisions.

To be like God, in his image, means that we are meant to live in association with each other. Our model for appropriate relationships with each other is found in the relationships within the Trinity. The Father, Son, and Holy Spirit live in harmony with each other and within God's self. That is, God is one essence in three persons, and peace and harmony characterize their relationship one with the other and in their unity or oneness. So, in God's image, you and I are meant to live with others in the same peace and harmony. Human marriage is meant to be the primary image which reflects our relationship with God. Marriage is intended as a lifelong, fully committed, exclusive, and loving relationship.

The image of God is exemplified by communication. There is an ongoing exchange between others and us. One of the surprising characteristics of God to me is his unending attempts to express himself to you and me. I don't understand why he would want to talk to me. The only reason I know is that he loves me.

Now don't just run by that phrase "he loves me." We have so tritely used this phrase and concept that we have robbed it of much of its meaning. I believe there is between the Lord and some of his children an affectionate caring kindness—love. But, biblically, to say that God loves us means that he wants the best for us in every situation in our lives, and wanting the best for us, he works without ceasing to bring about that good. This does not mean that we always get what we want, generally because what we want is not always best for us. Our Lord knows what is best for us because he is able to see not just yesterday and today but every future day in our lives. Therefore, his best for us does not always parallel what we think might be best. These are the situations when we would need to submit and obey even if we don't understand. As you can see, the *love* of God for us is bigger than just communication, but it is the heart of attempting to reach out to others in conversation.

Responsibility is also part of the image of God, for we are charged with the duty of what is called the cultural mandate. "Be fruitful and increase in number" is the mandate to recreate by regeneration and creating a people who fill the earth to bring glory and praise to God and blessing to each other.

Dominion Not Domination

The second duty given to being made in God's image is to exercise dominion over the creatures of the earth. Humankind is charged with the tending or husbanding of the earth and its creatures. The "subduing" of the earth in verse 28 indicates a similar idea that is expressed in God's ordering of the original creation in order to bring it to a productive and usable condition for the good of all.

To have dominion over the earth and the creatures does not mean to dominate them. In any situation, when dominion, which is grace given by God for the benefit of all, swerves into domination, then it becomes sin; grace becomes abused and turns into that which is hurtful and not expressive of the will of the creator. Dominion is the wise and proper rule of man regarding the universe under the direction of the Lord for the benefit of the ones being subdued that they too might bring honor to God.

Another word descriptive for dominion would be government. We are to govern the world around us for the glory of God.

The image of God at heart may perhaps be described as the perfect marriage of will and freedom. He who possesses absolute freedom deigns to share some of his freedom with the creatures of the world, chief among them is humankind. To do so is an exercise of will. And the will is the conscious determination to use one's freedom to be or to do what she or he chooses without coercion. For us, that freedom sadly means that we are free to make poor choices, and it behooves us to remember that whether our choices are poor or good, they produce results; that is, every choice brings about some consequence, and those consequences are capable of enhancing our freedom or encasing us within taller prison walls.

Perhaps this should come first regarding God's creation of us in his own image. The image is our awareness, our self-consciousness, our knowledge that we are and that such knowledge brings responsibility. And central to this awareness comes a bane and blessing. Part of the image is our ability to remember. Memory is a gift of God's grace which blesses and burns, for it provides us the ability to retain and recall experiential information so that we may change or repeat experiences according to will.

Man and Woman

Following the creation of humankind in the image of God, the text immediately and most notably characterizes humanity as male and female. That is, before the mandates for replenishing and ruling the earth, the signal point is made that mankind is relational and personal as sexual beings—male and female. Therefore, sexual differentiation is primary in the beginning of creation. Male and female are what God intended.

Gender or sexual category is not an accident of birth, but it is God's intention for humankind. And the remainder of Scripture will recognize that single females and single males do bear the image of God in its fullness; however, there is a completion, one for the other, in the proper relationship of woman and man. In the totality of the human experience, sexual relations bring a completion and fulfillment which will mirror the image of God in its fullness.

Secondly, female and male share equally and fully the image of God; one does so as male and the other as female.

Adam is the Hebrew word for mankind in verse 27. Then it becomes the name for the first man in chapter 2. Please follow closely; what is being said in the phrase "male and female he created them" is that God created a male "Adam" and a female "Adam." I say it this way to indicate the full equality of the female with the male. When Adam's wife is named in chapter 2, she is named Eve because she is honored as the mother of all humankind, yet she remained a female "Adam." All of this is to emphasize the equality of male and female and of Adam and Eve before the fall into sin.

The intention of God regarding the replenishing and ruling of his world by the male and female is that they are both fully the image of God and responsible for the mandates he gives them. In our world today, following the fall, we have gender inequality which is of course sinful and never intended by our loving Creator.

Thirdly, both female and male are responsible before God for the carrying out of the cultural mandates of replenishing and ruling the earth.

In summary, male and female complement each other and fulfill one another in their respective genders as they bear the image of God within themselves. Sexuality is deemed very good and as a most significant part of being human. Human sexuality is not mere reproduction, but its larger purpose, unlike the animals, is to fulfill the promise of God's covenant with us (Genesis 9:7-17). Part of the intent of human sexuality is relational enjoyment.

13

Reflecting on the Seventh Day

God saw all that he had made, and it was very good. And there was evening, and there was morning—the sixth day. Thus, the heavens and the earth were completed in all their vast array [and all the host of them]. By the seventh day God had finished the work he had been doing; so, on the seventh day he rested from all his work. Then God blessed the seventh day and made it holy, because on it he rested from all the work of creating that he had done. (Genesis 1:31; 2:1-3)

The Seventh Day

After the six days of creative activity on the part of God, we move to the seventh day to be told what God is doing or not doing now. In one sense, we have moved into the heavenly scene where God abides. It is not that God does not abide on the earth or that he ever did; it is that God is above and beyond the created realm, not subject to time, space, and matter because God is the creator of time, space, and matter.

In verse 2 of Genesis 1, the text tells us, "Now the earth was..." and proceeds to depict for us the creational scene. This creation extends through chapter 2:1 which concludes, "Thus the heavens and the earth were completed in all their vast array." Then we move to the seventh day, and the scene changes.

So on this seventh day we are told that

- God finished the work he had been doing

- God rested from all his work

- God blessed the seventh day

- God made the seventh day holy because he rested from the work of creating that he had done.

Theologians have generally concluded that this text applies to the Sabbath because the word rest is the root word for Sabbath and because the text expresses a sabbatical theme, the theme of physical, national, and spiritual rest, which is carried throughout Scripture.

In Israel's faith life of course, the Sabbath, the seventh day becomes the day of worship. In Israel's national life, the day of rest becomes associated with the promised land—the movement into the land of Canaan. When Israel occupies and governs Canaan, the nation has been granted its rest by the Lord. If you remember, in Genesis 12:1-3, the story is told of the Lord's call of Abram to follow him. Abraham is given no proof of protection, no proof of provision. All he is given is the implied promise by the Lord who calls him that he will be with him and the implicit demand that Abraham must trust him. In the Abrahamic covenant, he promised Abram that he would give him babies and a land in which to house them (the promised land) and make them a blessing to every nation on earth. That is, they would be the good-news bearers (gospel carriers) of God's love and forgiveness to a fallen world. So, the land of Canaan as the Israelite's home is a mighty symbol of God's fulfillment of rest for them.

Lastly, the seventh day rest is Christianized by the early believers who came from Judaism. In Christian thought, the Sabbath rest or God's rest or "today" represents the day of God's grace in salvation as well as the ultimate rest for those who trust in God: eternal life with him (Hebrews 4:1-11). Such thinking is reflected in the Genesis text because unlike the other six days which recount an evening and a morning followed by the number of the day, this day details no ending. It is an eternal day.

In some sense, all humankind since creation has continued to live in God's eternal day, the seventh day. It is quite similar in thought to the New Testament teaching that the world has been in the "last days" since the life and ministry, death and resurrection of Christ. The writer of Hebrews ties both thoughts neatly together in Hebrews 1.1-2. "In the past God spoke to our forefathers through the prophets at many times and in various ways, but "in these last days" [since Jesus]. He has spoken to us by his Son, whom he has appointed heir of all things, and through whom he made the universe." It is in this sense that all have lived since creation in the seventh day of rest and since Jesus, in the last days. Therefore, the seventh day is God's great day of grace and salvation mirrored in his rest from his works.

This day, secondly, relates the enjoyment of God in his work. He gives us an invitation to join him in this contemplation because the text offers this to us, though it is not specifically stated. The presentation of this scene is conditioned to help us think of a skilled, master craftsman who has completed a project and who now enjoys the beauty of his workmanship. Resting is the satisfaction that comes from the knowledge of a job well done. In this sense, God permits us to enjoy his creative grace in our labors and endeavors even as he did in the six days of creation. For whatever work we are chosen to do in our lives, we learn to do it for the glory of God and the advancement of his kingdom.

An alternate way to understand this text is, in addition to regarding it as the creation of the universe, to understand it as God constructing the world as his temple in which his people will come to worship him (Walton). With this idea, we would see God on the seventh day, pleased (blessed) by what he has accomplished and ready now to set the temple (created universe) in operation. So resting carries with it the ideas of satisfaction, completion, and perfection in preparation for future use as intended by the creator.

The Lord of the Sabbath

As God is the Lord of creation and of rest on the seventh day, the great Architect, the Master Craftsman of the universe, the Lord of the seventh day, so Jesus is the Lord of the Sabbath. In

St. Mark 2:28, the evangelist tells us that the Son of Man (Jesus's self-designation) is Lord of the Sabbath. This statement is made following Jesus's defense of the disciples who picked heads of grain to eat on the Sabbath and who then were criticized by the Pharisees. The point the Pharisees wanted to make was that Sabbath law—the way the Jews honored God on the Sabbath—did not permit such action. But Jesus countered with, "The Sabbath was made for man, not man for the Sabbath."

By this statement Jesus radicalizes the seventh day by informing us that the Lord invited us to share Sabbath rest with him. It is just not an enjoyment and satisfaction to him, but it will be for us when we realize that he made the Sabbath for us. The Sabbath is a gift of God's free grace as surely as is creation and redemption. But the Pharisees made the Sabbath burdensome with regulation and ritual. That was never God's intention. His intent was worship and appreciation of one's faith and God.

The good news of God's grace is this: Today, Sabbath rest and God's rest all find enfleshment and fulfillment in Jesus of Nazareth. Since you and I are in Christ, we are resting in him already, and I'm reminded of his words in Matthew 11:28–30, "Come to me, all you who are weary and burdened and I will give you "rest." Take my yoke upon you and learn from me, for I am gentle and humble in heart, and you will find "rest" for your souls. For my burden is easy and my yoke is light." In Jesus, we find the only perfect resting place; indeed, with St. Mark, we rejoice, "So the Son of Man is Lord even of the Sabbath."

The Finished Work

"By the seventh day, God had *finished the work* he had been doing..." Let's develop a biblical theme. Creation is the first great act of God's grace; redemption is the second. Perhaps we can also say that the day of re-creation or new creation is the third. Within these parameters, all of God's grace continues to operate. When God is finished with creation, he rests. Creation is finished, yet we know it is ongoing.

On the cross, Jesus received the wine vinegar on a stalk of the hyssop plant and *he said, "It is finished."* Then he died. Redemption was accomplished. The second great act of God's grace was done, yet we know redemption continues to work in and through us by the ongoing and fulfilling presence of the Holy Spirit.

The Christian journey will one day reach its appointed destiny for you and me. We shall stand in good company. Nearing the end of his life, Paul wrote Timothy 4:7,

I have fought the good fight, I have *finished the race*, I have kept the faith. Know there is laid up for me the crown of righteousness, which the Lord, the righteous Judge, will award me on that day, and not only to me, but also to all who have longed for his appearing.

"I have finished the race" sums up superbly the sentiment of the seventh day text. What that rest is to God, finishing the race is to Paul and to us. The joy of a life well-lived, having worked in the kingdom of the Lord, and finishing what was set before us, and that ministry to which we were called, then we enter into the rest of our Lord. John tells us, "Then I heard a voice from heaven say, ‚€~Write: Blessed are the dead who die in the Lord from now on." "Yes," says the Spirit, "they will 'rest' *from their labor*, for their deeds will follow them."

In Revelation 16:17, at the end of the bowls of wrath, God's last great attempt to impress his mercy, grace, and love upon those who will not follow him, "The seventh angel poured out his bowl into the air, and out of the temple came a loud voice from the throne, saying, *'It is done!'*" Then in deafening succession come the flashes of lightning, rumblings, peals of thunder, and a severe earthquake.

Creation is finished; redemption is finished. Mercy seen as judgment is finished. Now comes the end.

Then in Revelation 21:6, after the new Jerusalem descends from heaven, the old order has passed away, and everything is made new; the one seated on the throne said, "It is done." So the work of God is finished from creation to redemption to the new creation.

He said to me, "It is done. I am Alpha and Omega, the Beginning and the End. To him who is thirsty I will give to drink without cost from the spring of the water of life." (Revelation 21:6)

"Amen, even so come, Lord Jesus." (Revelation 22:20b)

14

Closing Thoughts on the Creator and Creation

As we bring our study of the first chapter of Genesis to a close, I want to share with you further reflections which I hope are beneficial to you.

Transforming Chaos

God does not destroy chaos; God transforms it and redeems it to suit his purpose. There is nothing nor anyone in God's created order who is expendable to him. Sometimes I look at people and situations I face in my life wishing that I could just simply not have to deal with them; that I could just walk away. And I may withdraw to a limited extent, but I never forget that the God who created and loves me created and loves those people for whom I feel disgust.

Each of us has within us a deep reservoir of chaos even though we are secure in the keeping of our Lord Jesus. Christians continue to sin, practice poor judgment, inflict injuries of the spirit and psyche, emotions, and will upon others. That is chaos continuing to express itself by twisting you and me and tempting us away from the image of the Lord implanted within us by the Spirit of God. It is fairly easy for us to find that ugly chaos in those around us; it is more difficult to find it in the soul mirror into which we look from time to time.

Indeed, we are victims of the residue of evil in the human condition generally and in our personal lives particularly. Illness and disease, pain and suffering, injustice and inequality are what we are bequeathed in life. It comes to us as part of our inheritance from the hand of Satan by way of the distortion of our choices to live life our way and to make ourselves captains of our own destinies.

All of this is a description of our spiritual condition which is *dis-ease*. We are not at ease; we do not find comfort and peace in our own skins. We are without doubt children of grace on the way to the Sabbath rest, yet at the very same time, we dance to the devil's tune far more often than we care to admit. I'm reminded of the exhortation of an old African-American preacher who admonished his congregation, "Don't ever give the devil a ride," he proclaimed, "he always wants to drive."

So, when we are pushed to distraction by the chaos we see in someone else's life and we are tempted to discard them, we need to remember that there have been many times the Lord would have liked to be rid of our shenanigans too. We each are broken vessels in our Master's service needing to be reminded that God never gives up on us. He never throws the clay away.

Empty and broken I came back to Him

A vessel unworthy—so scarred by my sin;

But He did not despair, He started over again;

And I bless the day He didn't throw the clay away.

"He is the Potter and I am the clay

Molded in His image He wants me to stay

When I stumble and fall and my vessel breaks

He just picks up the pieces,

He doesn't throw the clay away.

"Over and over He molds me and makes me

Into His likeness He fashions the clay.

A vessel of service I am today

All because Jesus didn't throw the clay away.

(Gene Reasoner)

The Love of God for His Creation

Throughout church history, there have been repeated movements which desired to denigrate the body, the material world, and all things human. Usually, these "spiritual" folks are libertines in Christian living; they enjoy the bodily pleasures without qualms because they contend God doesn't care about the body. He cares only for the spirit of humankind.

Sometimes, from Platonism, it goes so far as to teach that death is the liberation of the spirit from the body. This is not Christian teaching. For the Christian, death is the resurrection of the body and spirit bringing that person into the full expression of eternal life. Our bodies are not destroyed but transformed. That is not a comforting thought for those outside of Christ; their bodily existence continues too in a destructive state. We believe that the body is raised too in that final day and renewed, recreated, reformed with the spirit into the person God intended us to be from the beginning without the influence and effect of sin as well as the person God intends us to be throughout all eternity. In other words, I'm not saying that the body you have now is the body you will have in heaven, but I am saying that your body is precious to the Lord, and though scarred by sin, it will be transformed in that final day.

The almighty God, the creator, loves and cares for the created order. It is his world. He made it for us and made us to inhabit it and died to redeem us to live forever in his presence and for his glory. So, what is human, what is material, what is of this world is dearly loved by God. The supreme witness we have of God's love for this created order is that he sanctified it by coming into human life as a baby—a human body—to live and walk among us.

God could not have affirmed the creation any more strongly than by the birth, life, ministry, death, resurrection, and ascension of the bodily Jesus. As God, the eternal Son, Jesus sanctified, "holy-ized," human life in its richness and abundance. So far from denigrating the significance of the body, Christians believe that how we treat our bodies and the bodies of others around us is absolutely essential, and that one day, we shall be judged by those standards. Paul admonished the Corinthians (1 Corinthians 6:18–19),

Flee from sexual immorality... Do you not know that your body is a temple of the Holy Spirit, who is in you, whom you have received from God? You are not your own; you were bought at a price. Therefore, honor God with your body.

I heard a preacher recently in a local congregation, not a mega church, proclaim that most of us would turn away in disgust if someone suggested that we participated in the acts of the sinful nature listed in Galatians 5:10-21 by the Apostle Paul. They are "sexual immorality, impurity and debauchery; idolatry and witchcraft; hatred, discord, jealousy, fits of rage, selfish ambition, dissensions, factions and envy; drunkenness, orgies, and the like." These sins would not be characteristic of our lives, the preacher continued; then he concluded, but what is the difference when we watch them on television or at the movies? He then named two so-called "reality" shows. Christians must someday answer the question—how fully can Christians participate in culture and still participate in Christ? God loves what he has created and does not countenance its abuse in any form. It amazes me how concerned people can get over environmental issues without a sign of distress over moral and spiritual issues. Which is more important? The saving of a fish or one species or the reclaiming of a dis-eased, sinful woman or man for the kingdom of God?

Life Is Holy

One possible truth we may infer from the seventh day theology is that the first six days are secular time, and the seventh day is set aside as holy time. Thus, God establishes the framework for worship and rest. This truth could be more easily ascertained from the Deuteronomist's expansion of the fourth commandment (Deuteronomy 5:12–15). I have always been a bit uncomfortable with this thinking because it leads us to a division of life into secular and holy, ordinary and sacred.

It seems to me that the biblical representation of the Lord teaches that all life is holy to him. As I mentioned earlier, the Lord "holy-ized" all space, matter, and time by his creation and by his incarnation, life, death, and resurrection. Without doubt, in this world, there are some days and times set aside to be used in holy ways and some places hold special significance for our spiritual journeys because in those places, God spoke to us. But it seems to me that this division of space, matter, and time as secular or holy is not what God intended. If he did intend such a division, why does it not continue in the life to come?

Beyond death, in the fullness of eternal life, all will be holy, sanctified, preparing us for the worship of God and for service in his heavenly kingdom whereby we shall glorify him and enjoy him forever, which is the purpose of all human life. In the words of an old gospel hymn, "Every Day Will Be Sunday Bye and Bye." So, the ultimate goal of Christian living is to be holy as God is holy remembering the Lord's instruction of his people in Leviticus 19:2, "Be holy, because I, the Lord your God, am holy."

Creation Occurred on Sunday

I share this with you in fear and trepidation because I realize that the basic affirmation is not biblical, yet the premise still interests me. Because the description of the seventh day has been associated with the Sabbath, one could suppose that creation began on Sunday, Sunday being the day following Jewish Sabbath. Actually, this is not too far-fetched since the two accounts of the fourth commandment in the Ten Words, Exodus 20:11 and Deuteronomy 5: 12, offer the seventh day rationale as justification for the Sabbath, which was and is observed on Saturday. (So, if Saturday is day seven, then Sunday is day one.) God began his creation on Sunday.

The second biblical event, on which all of human history hinges, the most significant occurrence in time, is the resurrection of Jesus from the grave. Of course, without question, Jesus was raised on Sunday. All four of the evangelists (Mark, Matthew, Luke, and John) attest that the resurrection transpired very early on the first day of the week, Sunday. St. Mark writes, "When the Sabbath was over [Saturday]â€¦when the sun had risen..." So the general creation which was granted the grace of the first light of the presence of God in Genesis 1:3 occurred on Sunday as did the ultra-light of the resurrection of the man Jesus into God's victory over sin and death and the grave.

In Acts 2:1, we find the third act of sovereign grace occurring on Sunday in the creation of the church, the new Israel, on the day of Pentecost following Jesus's death and resurrection. Pentecost refers to the fiftieth day after the Sabbath of the Passover (Leviticus 2:.4-7, 15-16). The fiftieth day brings us to a Sunday. Moreover, Pentecost is also called the Feast of Harvest, and that initial day of Pentecost celebration is called the day of first fruits. St. Paul, in his magnificent treatise on the resurrection in 1 Corinthians 15, writes in verse 17 following:

And if Christ has not been raised, your faith is futile; you are still in your sins. Then those who have fallen asleep [died] in Christ are lost. If only for this life we have hope in Christ, we are to pitied more than all men. *But* Christ has indeed been raised from the dead, the first fruits of those who have fallen asleep.

Now, here is the other reason for my trepidation about this. If Sunday were the day the Lord chose to create the world, raise Jesus from the dead to eternal glory, and for the Spirit of God to descend to the believing disciples, creating them as the church of Jesus Christ, then I would suspect that the Lord Jesus will return on a Sunday as well inaugurating the victory of God over the forces of evil and instituting the rule of the kingdom of God where his will is certainly done on earth as it is in heaven.

Creation and Providence

God's creation is purposeful and ordered. God's creation is intentional, deliberate, and deliberated. There is nothing haphazard or ill-considered. God wills. God speaks. God sees. God pronounces it good. That same loving Father gives us direction for the ordering of our lives. We are not to be so deliberate or obstinate that we refuse to do anything, but we are reminded to think out our desires, our decisions before we begin our actions.

Providence is the belief that God's original purpose in creating will one day be realized and actualized in the lives of human beings and in the created order. Sin and evil will not be permitted to enjoy their partial reign over this world. This world belongs to God, and as Jesus fought the battles against Satan in the desert, in Gethsemane, on the cross, during death, and the darkness of the grave, one day, this world will once more be handed over to the Father.

Providence means to "see ahead" which means that because of the Father's omniscience and omnipotence and omni-agape all perfectly aligned, he has the power to permit the disobedience of his creatures and the rebellion of his creation because of the freedom in his image extended to humankind, and still be able, without force or compulsion, to finally accomplish his will and purpose in his world. His work in the past and present today is perfect work because, by his providence, he is able to see the future outcome of everyone and everything.

I believe in His loving providence with all my heart for all my life. This is very difficult at times. We have heartaches and illness, disease and situations which hurt us and bind us and from which we seem unable to extricate ourselves. Sometimes we cry, "O God, where are you?" Even if my cry seems weak, at the same time, I never doubt that God is with me and working for my good, no matter the limited vision I seem to have regarding the circumstances. God is always cooperating in the working out of human history to bring the best from adverse circumstances (Romans 8:28).

Our Father takes a personal interest in each of our lives, regardless the significance of the situation. This is the affirmation of Joseph who was sold into Egyptian slavery by his brothers, yet he rose to the heights of Egyptian power and eventually saved his starving brothers who sold him into slavery years before. "So, it was not you who sent me here, but God; and he made me a father to Pharaoh" (Genesis 45:8). Joseph saw beyond his circumstances and found the purpose of God in his life, and it transformed him; it made him a new man.

We see providence in Job's life. Maintaining accurately his innocence before God of the sins his friends suggested, he found his only vindication to be his hope for a redeemer (Job 19:25) in the future. His present was too p-r-e-s-e-n-t for him. He found no justice there. Yet he trusted in God's providence.

For you and me, the seeking of the will of God is our desire to participate in the providence of God. Just because we seek his will does not mean that all that happens is his will. God will honor human freedom and not our freedom alone or our freedom above everyone else's. In these times, we need to trust him because in his providence, he is working out all things for the best.

Prayer

Praying is our response to cooperate with the providence of the Lord in our lives. Praying is not talking about God as I hear some do today when they bow their heads; we have not prayed until we talk to God. The basic definition of prayer is being "toward God." We are not ever "toward God" unless we meet him in submission to his will and obedience to this word. When God knows that we have ceased to play games with him, that we have submitted, given up, and agreed to obey him, then God comes to us.

When we experience the presence of God, and these are the supreme moments in Christian living, then we can accept the providence of God, no matter what. Therefore, what the Lord God did "in the beginning," he will bring to realization in the end, for it is he who is "the Alpha and the Omega, the First and the Last, the Beginning and the End." In him, we find our perfect peace.

Concluding Encouragement

Remember, the purpose of this document is to encourage you to reflect for yourself on the written Word and the living Word, Jesus Christ, whom you find within it. I invite you to read some of what I have shared with you in reflecting as ongoing, continual meditation day by day. Ideally, you will reflect on what I might have written, and then go back to the Scripture being considered for the reflections the Spirit may have for you. I certainly have no monopoly on the Spirit of God. As I ask my congregation faithfully, why would you read the writings of another human being on Scripture when you have the original document before you? My teaching is not to ignore other fine Christian teachers and preachers, but do not underestimate what the Spirit of God may say to you.

Now, we must test our own reflections on Scripture. There is a great temptation into which many have fallen: the temptation to place their thinking on the same level as Scripture. But never will our experience be confirmed unless it agrees with the written Word of God informed by the Holy Spirit and the thinking and inspiration of other faithful Christian writers across the spectrum of time and theology. This is truth. The Holy Spirit will never give a child of God a thought or a theology which disagrees with the theology of the written Word. We must test our inspiration against that which we know to be inspiration indeed, affirmed by the church throughout the ages and the self-authenticating authority of the Scriptures.

About the Author

Randolph Kesler, an ordained Christian pastor, has served as pastor in Baptist and Presbyterian congregations for thirty years. He earned his Master of Divinity from Southeastern Baptist Theological Seminary in Wake Forest, North Carolina, and has done additional graduate work toward a master of theology.

Back Cover Summary

We Christians live in a rushed and hurried culture which our churches have accepted without thinking through the consequences. It seems that we have allowed ourselves to equate busyness with spirituality and bible study with the loudest opinion in the room.

Reflecting attempts to call us back to a matured time in Christian history when congregants did not read the Bible speedily. One of my high school English teachers used to warn us that just vocalizing words aloud was different than truly reading. This book calls us to read the Scripture, reread the Scripture, think about what we have read, and to meditate on the concepts of a passage following them throughout Scripture. By this means, we should be able to grasp a more complete understanding of the ideas the verses have presented to us.

Moreover, a slower reading and a rereading allows time for the Holy Spirit to speak to us. Often, I hear someone express that as often as they have read a certain passage of Scripture, they did not gain the newest understanding from their latest reading. Why is that?

It is because we have just called words without reflecting on them. Reflecting and meditating are old ways of studying the Word of God. You will be richly blessed by beginning and maintaining the practice. It is indeed food for the hungry Christian's soul.